PHOBIAS

The Crippling Fears

by Arthur Henley

with a Foreword by
Marshall P. Primack, M.D.

Lyle Stuart Inc. *Secaucus, New Jersey*

Library of Congress Cataloging-in-Publication Data

Henley, Arthur.
Phobias: the crippling fears.

Includes index.
1. Phobias--Popular works. I. Title.
RC535.H46 1987 616.85'225 87-7105
ISBN 0-8184-0425-6 (pbk.)

Published by Lyle Stuart, Inc.
120 Enterprise Ave., Secaucus, N.J. 07094
In Canada: Musson Book Company
A division of General Publishing Co. Limited
Don Mills, Ontario

Manufactured in the United States of America

to JANET with love

ACKNOWLEDGMENTS

I AM GRATEFUL to many people for their help in making this book possible. The names of some appear in these pages; the names of many others do not, nor is it possible to list them all.

But these include the dozens of men and women who allowed me into their private lives so that I could capture their personal stories, and afforded me opportunities to test the hundreds of innovative, fear-fighting, self-help strategies that you will find described in these pages.

My special thanks to all the experts who shared with me their time and expertise. Their generous cooperation made possible a book that reflects not merely a single point of view but that of many different disciplines in the field of phobia, anxiety and panic disorders so that *every* reader may find here valuable, usable insights into his or her phobic fears and a variety of proven ways to deal with them.

My own experience as a self-cured phobic gave me particular insight into the difficulties encountered by anyone who suffers from one or another of the crippling fears.

And a final word of thanks to the people at Smith Corona for introducing me to the magic of word processing. Their PWP System 14 personal word processor not only made writing easier—it cured my *"techno-phobia"*!

Contents

PART THREE

Phobia Resource Directory

The cases described are real but except where noted names and other identification have been changed to protect the subject's privacy.

Foreword

PHOBIAS, panic disorders and anxiety attacks affect millions of otherwise normal, healthy men and women. I have seen in my own medical practice how seemingly inconsequential fears can grow to terrifying proportions and dominate a person's life.

In this soundly researched comprehensive book, the author uses vivid case histories and illuminating interviews with experts in the field to demonstrate the destructive impact of these crippling fears, from agoraphobia to cancerphobia. He emphasizes the importance of distinguishing such problems from cardiac, thyroidal and other illnesses.

Every kind of phobia is described, simply and clearly, to help the reader recognize its characteristic symptoms. In an easy, conversational style that is both instructive and engrossing, the author discusses in depth the origin of phobias and what to do about them.

Whatever it is that you're afraid of, and to whatever degree—be it flying, closed spaces, open spaces, elevators, bridges, sex, traffic, other people, shopping malls, and so on—you will find it described here in these pages and learn how to use the treatment that works best for you.

This book will be an eye-opener for those not aware of these problems and will prove extremely useful to those who suffer from these conditions.

The reader will discover that a phobia is not necessarily a single phenomenon treatable by a single technique. But while there is no one way to free everyone from a phobia, panic disorder, or crippling anxiety, there *is* a way to treat *every* phobic problem.

Every reader will learn how to find and use the treatment that works best for himself or herself. The techniques described here include a wide range of practical self-help coping strategies, relaxation exercises and authoritative treatment methods employed by specialists in phobias, panic disorders and anxiety-related syndromes.

A number of carefully designed self-tests help the reader come to grips with his or her phobic problem, and professional insights from phobia experts spell out directions on safe, dependable ways to eliminate phobias.

An extensive nationwide resource directory guides the reader to professionals, clinics and support groups specializing in phobias and panic disorders, and highlights new advances in phobia research. The detailed index gives quick and easy access to specific information on all aspects of phobic distress and treatment.

By reading this book, anyone who suffers from phobias will have taken a giant step to overcoming these fears.

—MARSHALL P. PRIMACK, M.D.
Director of Internal Medicine
New York State Psychiatric Institute,
Columbia-Presbyterian Medical Center

PHOBIAS
The Crippling Fears

PART ONE

HOW PHOBIAS TAKE CONTROL
(The Problem)

Chapter 1

The Panic Button

BUGS.

Nobody likes them.

We swat them, spray them, step on them.

Beetles, ants, flies, moths, mosquitoes, roaches. Especially roaches.

Phyllis J., now twenty-eight, always had a strong dislike for roaches. Whenever she saw one, she reached quickly for something to hit it with. A newspaper, her shoe, anything she could lay her hands on. If she got it, she scooped it up in a tissue and flushed it down the toilet. If she missed, it slipped away and simply vanished. And that was that.

Until one evening, after she'd gone to bed but was unable to go to sleep because she felt thirsty. So she got up to get a glass of water. She went into the kitchen, turned on the light and approached the sink.

Suddenly, a huge black cockroach darted out of nowhere and sped across the drainboard. Phyllis froze in terror. The glass dropped from her hand and shattered in the sink.

She screamed, and couldn't stop screaming. Her heart pounded, her body shook all over, and she gripped the drainboard apron to steady herself in case she should faint.

Her screams awakened her husband from his half-sleep and he came running to her side. He took her trembling body in his arms, pleading, "What happened? Please try to calm down and tell me what happened."

Gradually, held tightly in his arms, she settled down and regained her ability to speak. Pointing to the sink, she said in a husky voice, "I saw a roach."

"What? That's all?" he replied incredulously. "Why didn't you reach for the insect spray?"

"I couldn't. I just couldn't. I don't know why. It isn't the first roach I've seen but this time it was different. Something came over me. I was scared to death."

"The roach must have crawled across your hand. That's why you were so frightened."

"No," she said. "The roach didn't come anywhere near me. It disappeared into the woodwork, I guess. I was too spaced-out to notice."

Her puzzled husband shook his head in disbelief. "It must have been the shock of seeing it that scared you so," he said, "and not the roach itself."

It seemed a reasonable enough assumption but, as Phyllis was to learn, reason alone is insufficient to cure the victim of a panic attack. That traumatic experience was only the beginning of a lifestyle so crippled by phobic fear that she later described her every living moment as "Hell, life is just plain hell!"

After her panic attack, Phyllis would not enter her kitchen at night unless her husband preceded her, turned on the light and checked out the place for roaches.

But her fear didn't stop there. On the contrary, it grew. She began to avoid not only her dark kitchen but also any room that was dark and, soon after, all enclosed places—closets, phone booths, elevators. Then it was buses. Then it was theaters, and restaurants, and shopping malls. She reached a point where she could not bear to be left alone in the examining room at her doctor's office.

Ultimately, she became so closed in by her grossly expanded fear that she was unable to venture outside her home. And all night, every night, she insisted on leaving at least a small light burning in every room. She so dreaded the thought of seeing a roach anywhere that she commenced to inspect the telephone before she answered its ring or made a call.

Her *entomophobia* (fear of bugs) had progressed to *agoraphobia* (fear of leaving the safety of home). She was paying her dues in a catastrophic way for the "privilege" of belonging to a very special "club" of some 40 million American men and women who suffer—underscore that word *suffer*—from phobias of various kinds and of varying severity.

"The impact on an individual's life can be every bit as severe as multiple sclerosis or paraplegia," says Dr. Robert L. DuPont, Jr., a Georgetown University psychiatrist and the founding president of the Phobia Society of America.

While not everyone who is afraid of bugs will push the panic button, the effects of such fear can be just as devastating mentally, physiologically and socially. This happens because both mind and body rev up in response to a danger that doesn't actually exist. The danger is inside of you, not outside of you.

When you have a phobia, you feel terribly threatened not because you are actually threatened but simply because you feel threatened. It is more than just fear. It is terror, dread and, sometimes, panic.

Someone said that trying to explain a phobia to a non-phobic person is like trying to explain pregnancy to a man.

But Just Imagine . . .

That someone is pointing a loaded gun at your head, his finger wrapped around the trigger, and threatening to blow your brains out.

If you keep your eyes closed and there are no distractions, the visual image of being trapped and in danger of having your head blown off will send your body reeling. Your heart will pound, your adrenaline will start pumping and the sweat will rise in the palms of your hands.

Or let your imagination conjure up this mind-picture, different but no less terrifying. Imagine yourself being buried alive. You can feel the dirt being thrown on top of you, suffocating you as it closes your mouth and fills your nostrils.

This powerful image will surely cause you to breathe hard, perhaps even hyperventilate, as well as triggering the symptoms mentioned previously.

Now you know what a panic attack feels like. You know something about the sheer terror produced by a phobia. You have experienced the awesome, debilitating effects of the thought alone on your brain, your nervous system and your body chemistry.

But nothing really happened!

There was no gun at your head. You weren't being buried alive. At no time was there any real threat to your well-being. Only your thoughts were out of control. That is the essence of a phobia.

It stretches your mind beyond normal, everyday anxiety that may indeed prompt some concern for your safety. You may, for example, have read that a bridge collapsed somewhere. That could provoke a certain amount of concern about driving your car across a similar bridge.

But if you are truly phobic about bridges, you will experience a degree of dread that is wholly out of proportion to reality. Any bridge will trigger feelings of terror. More to the point, such feelings will take hold of you in mere contemplation of driving across a bridge.

No real danger exists, or if it does, it is very slight. But your mind perceives it otherwise. Your brain sends a three-alarm signal to your body. That's when you push the panic button.

However, just as mind-pictures of the kind described can mobilize what is called a fight-or-flight response to danger, even falsely perceived danger, so too can mind-pictures be employed to work for you to overcome your phobia. In this book you will learn how to use this powerful tool, and other equally powerful techniques, to establish a sense of control over self-destructive thoughts and the crippling fears they arouse.

The need for a variety of phobia-fighting techniques is necessary because . . .

All Phobics Are Not Alike

It is generally acknowledged by experts in the field that people most vulnerable to phobias are distinguished by a high degree of emotional sensitivity. They are generally very bright, imaginative, and endowed with hair-trigger nervous mechanisms that respond to anxiety-provoking stimuli more intensely than does the average person.

Women are more sensitive than men. Agoraphobia is more prevalent among females than among males. So-called "simple" phobias—specific irrational fears that can be managed by avoiding the thing one fears, be it a cockroach, an elevator or a pussy cat—also afflict more females than males. And no matter what the source may be, women are more likely than men to push the panic button.

What accounts for this difference between the sexes?

Some suspect it may have to do with a difference in the blood flow rate in the brain, and in the nerve connections between the brain's left and right hemispheres. Because these elements differ in males and females, they could affect the way the sexes respond emotionally to the very same stimuli.

There are also hormonal differences and cultural differences, and one may influence the other so that the two sexes perceive the world differently. No one can dispute the fact that, historically, different standards were set for boys and girls. Boys were raised to be dominant, unemotional and competitive; girls were raised to be attractive, nurturing and compliant.

These differences, while making women more vulnerable to phobias, can make male phobics more vulnerable to the destructive effects of their phobias.

Dr. Michael R. Liebowitz, Director of the Anxiety Disorders Clinic at New York State Psychiatric Institute, has observed, "Given the same anxiety attacks, I've found that women more readily tend to become house-bound, whereas men may instead turn to alcohol."

Plainly, what he means is that female agoraphobics avoid panicking by staying home while male agoraphobics subdue their panic attacks by drowning their fear in drink. Their first concern is to protect their self-image.

But even phobics of the same sex, and afflicted by the same phobia, differ in the ways they react to whatever it is they're afraid of. Some may push the panic button; others may find sufficient resources within themselves to keep functioning despite suffering an enormous degree of anxiety.

The fear of flying offers an excellent case in point. It is no exaggeration to suggest that all, or almost all, phobics are anxious to some degree about airplanes. Captain Tom Bunn, a pilot himself, runs a workshop for fearful fliers called SOAR (Seminars On Aeroanxiety Relief), and says, "There's a natural tendency to be fearful where you have no escape, as on an airplane, and different people have different ways of handling their fear."

Sometimes the means chosen to handle it are very surprising as he makes clear in relating . . .

The Curious Case of the Airborne Aerophobic

She was attractive, in her middle thirties and recently divorced. Her name, for this account, shall be Amanda. She held an executive position with an international corporation that necessitated frequent flights abroad. Although childless and otherwise unbound by familial responsibilities, her need to fly posed a great burden because she suffered from aerophobia. Only the more urgent need, or drive, to keep her job enabled her to cope with the sense of panic that invariably rose in her throat whenever she was forced to fly.

Now she had managed to control her fear sufficiently to board the plane at New York's JFK Airport, endure the anxiety accompanying take-off and settle back for the flight to Paris. But she could not shake off the anxiety that still plagued her.

Desperate for emotional support to head off her fear of fainting, Amanda turned to the man sitting beside her, a perfect stranger, and asked—no, implored—in a tremulous voice, "Please . . . Please . . . may I hold your hand while this plane is gaining altitude? I'm so frightened."

Startled, but not displeased, the stranger complied gladly, and noted that his companion seemed more relaxed now that they held hands.

She just sat there, seemingly content, saying nothing, until the plane hit an air pocket and the ride became bumpy. Each bump increased her anxiety.

"Please . . . oh, please," she said, "would you put your arm around me? I know it's an absurd request, we don't even know each other, but I'm scared to death!"

He smiled and, again, complied gladly. He was a man in his fifties, well-groomed, well-mannered, clearly successful, and most certainly relished the situation. He tried to make conversation but she was not very responsive. That is, not conversation-wise.

However, the flight became extremely rocky, and this exacerbated Amanda's fear. She was in a kind of dream-like state when she laid her head upon his shoulder, murmuring, "Oh, God, you're the most wonderful, the most important person in my life."

Thus, Amanda endured the flight, her head resting on his shoulder while he held her close and patted her consolingly. It was a flight that he hated to see come to an end.

Well, the flight did come to an end. The plane landed safely and the two of them walked down the exit ramp together. When she turned to him to say goodbye, he smiled and asked her to join him for dinner.

Amanda drew back angrily. She seemed a completely different person. "I'll do no such thing!" she snapped. "How dare you make a pass at me! You are nothing to me. I haven't the slightest interest in ever seeing you again!"

She stalked off, leaving him to stare at her in absolute bewilderment. What he didn't know, and she didn't realize, was that once she was back on the ground the last shred of her anxiety had vanished and the memory of that flight had vanished with it.

Amanda was back on track again, flying high in spirit if not in fact, and her mind was on business, not pleasure. She had regained control of herself and her circumstances.

To people like Amanda, a phobia can be more inconvenient than incapacitating. But phobias play no favorites. Anyone is fair game. That includes you, your spouse or lover, your child, your parent, your best friend, your boss and, of course, some of your favorite people.

These are not celebrated phobics but, shall we say . . .

Phobic Celebrities?

If you've ever had a panic attack or simply have had to make changes in your lifestyle to contend with a phobia of one kind or another, you have a lot of company. Good company.

It may surprise you to learn that one of America's most-travelled persons, President Ronald Reagan, is reported to have been extremely anxious and fearful about flying during his acting career. But motivated by his need to campaign throughout the state of California in his bid to become Governor, he was able to overcome what may be called a "touch" of aeraphobia. If he still suffers from any residual anxiety, it is certainly not apparent from the confident steps he takes to and from Air Force I, as the TV camera has made clear.

Singer Aretha Franklin is another celebrated person who at times is in the grip of aerophobia. She is said to have canceled several appearances at times when her anxiety level was too high for her to cope with flying and there was no other alternative.

Perhaps the most famous aerophobe of all is John Madden, the former National Football League coach who led the Oakland Raiders to many championships and who is now a prominent TV broadcaster and actor in TV commercials. He is unusual in that he's been able to pursue a demanding career successfully in spite of the limitations imposed by his phobia. He avoids flying by taking trains or other land transportation.

Few can manage their jobs, or their lives, effectively by avoiding a fear of flying just by not flying when travel by other means is enormously inconvenient. Most, like Amanda, control their anxieties any way they can and fly anyway.

One such person is Phil Donahue, the popular host of his own TV show. "The more I fly, the more anxious I am," he told his viewers on one program, and then went on to give some fascinating insight into the phobic's need to maintain control.

"I will not read or do anything on take-off or landing," he said. "I have to help this pilot! If I don't concentrate . . . well, I can only speculate on how many landings I have successfully made around the world!"

The reluctance to give up control is a key characteristic of phobia. Maintaining even the illusion of control can be helpful as Phil Donahue's comment—ad-libbed, incidentally—makes clear.

Another well-known personality, TV weatherman Willard Scott, readily admits, "I am a phobic. It's nothing to be ashamed of, any more than diabetes or tennis elbow."

He told an overflow audience at the 1984 National Phobia Conference in Washington, D.C., that he suffered his first panic attack many years ago while crossing a bridge, reminding his listeners, "We are not alone. Help is available."

It is indeed. All kinds of help. All kinds are necessary because what will do for one will not do for another. You will see this more clearly as you continue reading and will learn how to apply what you read to cure your own phobia or that of someone close to you.

You may be heartened to learn that even Sigmund Freud was not immune from anxiety and phobia. He suffered from cardiac neurosis, which is another way of saying that he was phobic about having a heart attack despite the lack of any medical evidence of such a possibility. He also dreaded trains, but when travel by rail could not easily be avoided, he travelled that way, taking his luggage—and his anxiety—along with him.

The most celebrated phobic of our time was probably the late Howard Hughes. He was a *mysophobe,* a person inordinately fearful of germs, and wore gloves when it became necessary to shake hands with anyone. But in advancing years his fears became overwhelming and took control of his life.

He became an *agoraphobe,* refusing to go out, and ultimately he became a total *panophobe,* fearful of everyone and everything. Some saw him as nothing more than a hypochondriac, someone with constant complaints about imaginary ills. But the real root of his nature sprouted from a phobic seed that was most likely planted at birth, according to some theories, and influenced by environmental forces for which he had no useful coping strategies.

One of the most damaging coping strategies that phobics turn to is alcohol. This is clear to anyone who has seen a performance of Eugene O'Neill's play *The Iceman Cometh,* which takes place in a saloon where everyone is agoraphobic.

O'Neill names it "The Last Chance Saloon" and its proprietor is a man called Harry Hope, the last name being one of the great ironies in the drama. All the saloon's residents and Harry Hope himself never leave the premises. They have rooms upstairs and they drink downstairs.

As the play proceeds, it becomes clear that all are desperately fearful of leaving the saloon. Drinking until they pass out, they use booze to keep their phobias at bay and non-threatening, but otherwise intact. The booze doesn't extinguish their fear, but only conceals it.

The kind of fear we make reference to here goes far beyond the exercise of ordinary caution that alerts us, for example, to look both ways before we cross the street. In phobias, the fear is in the mind of the beholder and not in the circumstance itself.

When FDR presided over this nation during the great depression, he said, "The only thing we have to fear is fear itself."

In that memorable speech, he was not suggesting that we have no need for rational concern about surviving in a time of high unemployment, but that we must take care to check that concern. If left unchecked, our anxieties would surely build to a degree that would stifle our attempts to deal realistically with our problems.

Realistic fear can actually be a spur to achievement. It can be an incentive. Take it from a pro football Hall of Famer, Hugh McElhenny, who was known as "King of the Halfbacks" when he broke running records during his long career with the San Francisco Forty-Niners and other NFL teams.

"I ran scared all the time," he admitted. "My attitude was fear. Not the fear of being hurt, but the fear of being tackled, of being pulled down from behind, of being *embarrassed* in front of my teammates."

To him, "running scared" meant running away from possible humiliation and running towards a goal—a first down or a touchdown. Fear was the spur that drove him on. It was healthy, positive and appropriate. He was motivated, not demoralized.

Phobic fear is something else.

Queen Noor, the wife of King Hussein of Jordan, is Lisa Halaby, whose father was the head of the Federal Aviation Administration and chairman of Pan American World Airways. In her early years, when she was striving for personal success, she refused to accept a job from her famous and influential father, saying "I had a phobia about depending on him. I wanted to work on my own merits."

A phobia?

Hardly. That's using the word too loosely. She surely didn't mean that she had a distorted perception of danger in approaching her father for a job. She was simply reluctant to make herself dependent on him.

As any phobic knows, there is more to a phobia than merely being reluctant to confront what one is afraid of. Moreover, mere reluctance will never lead one to the terrifying experience of a panic attack.

Then again, phobia experts know that someone might push the panic button for no apparent reason. There may not be a roach or other intimidating creature in sight.

"A panic attack has a life of its own," says Dr. Thomas Uhde, a phobia specialist with the National Institute of Mental Health. "It can occur when persons aren't stressed at all. They could be content and still have a profound panic attack, even be awakened from sleep with one."

That kind of panic attack occurs spontaneously, seemingly without provocation. It just happens, and can happen anywhere . . .

Even in a Barber Chair

"I didn't just think I might die. I felt I was actually dying right then and there!"

That's how Victor explains the rush of intense terror that scrambled his mind when he had his first spontaneous panic attack at age nineteen.

It happened in a three-man barber shop of the "old-fashioned" kind, just a few blocks from his home, and was one he had visited many times before because he felt comfortable there. The barber who took care of him was not talkative. Neither was Victor. He considered the need to get a haircut a big bother and was eager to get the matter over with as quickly as possible.

Still, nothing unusual had ever happened. He sat still, obediently responding to the barber's occasional instruction to "Sit up, please" or "Don't move your head, please."

Sometimes, Victor closed his eyes, his mind blank, and listened to the clip-clip of the shears. Other times, he let his mind wander to thoughts of plans he was making for that evening. When the haircut was concluded and the barber had brushed stray hairs from his neck, he got off the chair, paid the barber and gave him a generous tip and an approving smile.

But not this time. He never reached that point. About five minutes into the haircut, he became gripped by an overwhelming sense of panic.

He couldn't catch his breath. His heart pounded furiously. His legs felt like jelly. He had cramps in the pit of his stomach.

"I felt something go in my brain," he says, recalling the experience.

"I was dying, really dying. I knew it wasn't real, it couldn't be real, and yet it *was* real. I wasn't thinking, I was feeling. I'm dying in this barber chair, that's what I was feeling. It was the most terrifying thing that ever happened to me. My life depended on my getting out of there as fast as I could!"

He tore the barber cloth from his neck, flung it aside and literally tumbled out of the chair, mumbling, "I'm sick, I'm sick. I have something to do."

The first remark was true. The second was a cover-up for his embarrassment.

"It's uncanny," he says now. "Despite this tremendous sense of panic, I maintained enough reasoning ability to feel embarrassed."

Once he left the barber shop and was out into the street, the panic began to subside. Its limits had been reached in the barber chair. He walked home as quickly as he could, hoping he would not meet anyone who knew him. Luckily, he did not. When he reached his home, he poured himself a glass of orange juice, his hands still trembling, and sat down in his favorite armchair. Within ten minutes, the last residue of panicky feelings was gone.

Victor never again returned to that barber shop except to pay the barber, give him an exceedingly generous tip and mumble some foolish excuse for his previous behavior.

For a while he tried to avoid going to barber shops by trimming his own hair. He found this difficult to do and not very becoming. So he sought out the smallest, most nondescript shops he could find, presided over by a lone barber, and dared to patronize him only when the shop was empty of other customers.

He always tells the barber, "I'm in a rush, I have an important appointment, so just give me a quick trim." He does not allow the barber cloth to be fastened around his neck, preferring whatever stray hairs may fall through his shirt collar to what he describes as "having a noose around my neck." Beneath the cloth his hands grip the cold arms of the barber chair for comfort. And he keeps tranquilizers in a shirt pocket "just in case," even though he knows they cannot possibly have an immediate effect.

Naturally, one of the first things Victor did after recovering his equilibrium was to consult his doctor for an explanation of the incident and a diagnosis.

The doctor examined him, checked his blood pressure and took an electrocardiogram.

"Just as I suspected," the doctor told him. "All the tests are negative. You have nothing but an old-fashioned anxiety neurosis, what used to be called neuro-circulatory aesthenia. I'll give you a pill to calm your nerves."

Why did his nerves lose their calm so suddenly and so precipitously? The doctor didn't know.

So Victor consulted another doctor, a psychiatrist. In the course of their conversation, Victor reiterated the fact that he never did like getting a haircut. He recalled that even as a small child, his mother had to hold him while the barber tried to cut his hair.

And, yes, he did indeed remember crying bitterly and weaving his head about to avoid the scissors. And the more he tried to escape, the tighter his mother held him to protect him from being nicked by the scissors, as she told him.

The diagnosis was clear. Childhood trauma, probably repeated many times until it became learned behavior, and a consequence of old long-buried feelings ("Oh, how you must have hated your mom!") being repressed. It all spilled over in the barber chair on that eventful day.

"I recommend psychoanalysis," the doctor told him, "or at least some form of psychotherapy."

Victor said okay, he'd try psychoanalysis. Over a period of several weeks he learned a great deal about himself—that he was a perfectionist, among other things, and that people who are perfectionists are more likely to become phobics—and insight piled upon insight during his analysis.

But one day he had another panic attack, just as devastating as the first one, although it occurred in a completely different situation. It happened in the movies when Victor was having a really good time and enjoying the picture immensely. He couldn't understand what it was that came over him.

So he consulted another specialist, this time one whose expertise was nutrition.

After performing a number of tests and checks of Victor's blood sugar levels, the doctor decided that the problem was hypoglycemia. His body was pumping adrenaline to compensate for sudden drops in his blood sugar. The solution was diet.

Victor agreed to try the diet. He hated to give up the fast-food emporiums that seemed to give him a bigger mental boost than an apple or an orange, but his dread of having another panic attack made him stick to his diet.

But he did have another panic attack. Again, it came on suddenly and inappropriate to the situation.

Still, this is not to say that all the doctors Victor had consulted were wrong. Chances are that if he were a woman, he may have been diagnosed as having PMS (PreMenstrual Syndrome), because all the symptoms that he presented to *all* the doctors he consulted could be indicative of precisely the problems that they diagnosed.

Phobias and panic attacks do indeed confound the experts, especially in view of the fact that there has been a spectacular rise in these disorders. Every year, doctors, mental health centers and phobia clinics report more people seeking their help.

In fact, phobia is now ranked above even depression and alcoholism as the most common mental health problem in the nation by many of the leading authorities and organizations in the mental health profession.

The good news is that there are now more and better ways of diagnosing, treating and curing phobias of every kind as well as the panic attacks that frequently accompany them.

And there is even better news. If you're a phobic, there are many things *you* can do to help *yourself,* as you will discover in the pages that follow.

Always bear in mind that a phobic lifestyle is a crippling lifestyle. Don't allow yourself to become a prisoner of fear, or, more to the point, inappropriate fear. One way to head off this possibility is to get a handle on the kind, and degree, of symptoms you experience when confronted by whatever it is that you fear or that provokes a panic attack.

If you're phobic, you're fearful, and if you're fearful, you're a worrier. So here and there throughout this book you will find a number of self-tests devised for "worry warts" to help you pinpoint and resolve these worries.

Make them into a game if you like, but don't take them any less seriously. They are carefully and scientifically devised to help you zoom in on phobic fears and their effects upon your mind, your body and your ability to cope with the stresses of everyday life.

Here is a *Worry Chart* that will help you fine-tune your perception of anxiety-producing stimuli that trigger . . .

A Laundry List of Symptoms

You may not be aware or ever really learn what set off a panic attack, but you will know for sure that you did indeed have one by the symptoms it produces. For an unpredictable period—anywhere from a few minutes to a few hours—you will suffer from acute physical and emotional distress.

Moreover, these symptoms will not be the result of physical exertion, drug use, medical problems or exposure to a truly life-threatening situation.

Here is a list of twelve key symptoms. Check those that you've experienced to an acute degree in the course of what you consider a panic attack . . .

Palpitations	______
Shortness of breath	______
Chest discomfort	______
Choking sensation	______
Unsteadiness	______
Sweating	______
Feeling of faintness	______
Trembling	______
Fear of going crazy or dying	______
Feeling of unreality	______
A strange tingling	______
Hot or cold flashes	______

If you checked at least four of these twelve symptoms, you can assume that you experienced a genuine panic attack, according to diagnostic standards set by the American Psychiatric Association.

Furthermore, if you experienced such attacks at least *three times in a three-week period,* you would be diagnosed psychiatrically as having *panic disorder.* That is a condition emanating from a misguided nervous system that sets off an alarm when no alarm is called for because no real threat, no danger, no risk exists.

Panic disorder, sometimes called anxiety disease, is a phobic phenomenon that has plagued people everywhere for hundreds of years but has only recently been recognized as a very special kind of phobic disorder.

If you think you have it, don't be concerned. It is very treatable by a number of means including some remarkable anti-panic pills and a host of other non-drug techniques.

Most phobias do not lead to the devastating feelings of an extreme panic attack, the absolute conviction that one is losing all control of himself or herself, or the situation at hand.

Nevertheless, the worry, apprehensiveness and anxiety can rise to a degree that triggers almost unbearable physical and emotional symptoms. Unlike a panic attack, a purely phobic attack can be *avoided* by simply staying away from the source of one's fear.

The less one avoids, and the closer one approaches, the source of that fear—no matter how unrealistic or irrational it may be—the more intensely will that person experience all sorts of symptoms.

Here is a more generalized list of phobic symptoms, some of them expressed in idiomatic terms because many phobics often describe them that way.

Look over this list. Have you experienced any of these symptoms? Often? Severely? Put down one check if you have ever experienced such feelings. Put down two checks if you have experienced them often or severely. . . .

Feeling shaky	______
Sudden stomach cramps	______
Rubbery legs	______
Have to urinate	______
Unable to swallow	______
Coughs on own spittle	______
Can't catch breath	______
Got to get out of here	______
Nerves are all shot	______
This is it	______

Just can't think straight	______
Nothing feels right	______

Surprise! You don't have to add up your check-offs. It makes little difference how many of these symptoms you checked *once* because they are very common . . . we all have some of them some of the time perhaps because we're all a little anxious, but these feelings do not really interfere with the way we conduct our lives.

However, if you made *two* checks next to a number of these symptoms, you may fall short of pushing the panic button but are probably more phobic than is comfortable, and certainly more phobic than is good for you.

You are treading a fine line between the good life and the phobic life.

If the latter, you may be only a step and jump away from sheer terror, from phobias that terrorize and cripple.

Yes, cripple.

Please turn the page. . . .

Chapter 2

The Crippling Fears

IS THE GLASS half-full or half-empty?

The optimist will reply, "It's half-full. Look at all that's left."

But the pessimist will reply, "It's half-empty. Soon there'll be nothing left."

The phobic is a pessimist, at least in terms of his or her phobia. Always, the worst is yet to come. . . .

"Sure, the bridge is holding up now, but with just one more car on it, who knows? What if that car is my car? What if that's all it takes to make the bridge collapse?"

"Don't misunderstand me, Doctor. It's not that I don't trust your competence as a surgeon. But things can happen. What if your hand slips? What if you have a heart attack in the middle of the operation?"

"I know that using a condom will prevent my getting pregnant or getting AIDS. But what if it breaks? And what if this is my most fertile time and your sperm is right on target?"

Three phobics, all suffering from a case of the "what ifs." That is the hallmark of the phobic and that is why phobia is often referred to as the disease of the "what ifs."

If phobics are sure of anything, they're sure that the worst will happen and anticipate the approaching debacle with a feeling of certainty. "What if" becomes equivalent to "I'm damned sure it will!"

Forever anticipating the worst, it's no wonder that the phobic is always anxious, nervous, on the alert when faced with the possibility of having to confront the source of the phobia. He is like a soldier doing sentry duty, never allowed to leave his post lest something happen.

It's a matter of staying prepared, keeping watch, waiting fearfully to get hit by the "big one."

The only way out of the sentry post is to avoid whatever it is that got them there in the first place. Don't go near that bridge, postpone surgery, skip sex . . . that's what the three phobics mentioned previously have to do.

Clearly, such avoidance does far more than merely cramp one's style. It could prevent you from getting from place to place because if you don't cross the bridge there's no other way to get there. It could sharply increase your risk of dying because the operation you put off could mean the difference between life and death. It would certainly deprive you of one of life's greatest pleasures and probably make you miserable if you regarded sexual relations as threatening rather than as a joyous celebration of life.

And every time you avoid the thing you fear, you reinforce the phobia. Avoidance piled upon avoidance adds up to a truly crippling fear.

Why?

Because you have made a habit out of your fear. Avoiding the source of that fear will have become a knee-jerk reaction, an automatic unstoppable response.

Sheer terror can become so overwhelming that you can actually smell it. That is no exaggeration. Take it from one of the American hostages in the Iranian take-over of the U.S. Embassy during Jimmy Carter's presidency. Following his release, he said that there were times when "you could actually smell the fear!"

No phobic knows the smell of fear more keenly than the one who suffers from the most restrictive fear of all . . .

Agoraphobia

If anyone can be called a prisoner of fear, it is the agoraphobe, a person who becomes terror-stricken at the thought of leaving the safety of home. And because it generally occurs during the most productive years of one's life, between ages 25 to 45, its effects worm their way into the social, marital and work-related aspects of the victim's day-to-day existence.

In her very moving autobiographical book, *Afraid of Everything: A Personal History of Agoraphobia,* Daryl M. Woods wrote, "It produces a personal wasteland from which each individual must try to reclaim himself."

Or herself . . . because, for reasons suggested in the previous chapter, most agoraphobes tend to be women. However, one cannot place too much emphasis on statistics. It is not unlikely that more women than men seek professional help, and that's the source from which statistics on this subject are derived. Also, since the majority of women are neither liberated nor employed, they may find it easier than men to remain housebound. Agoraphobe or not, the average man must get to work despite the enormity of his anxiety.

The agoraphobia may have been brought on by a panic attack that came without warning, spontaneously, or in response to a frightening stimulus. It really may not have presented a threat at all but it was perceived to be a threat, and that's what phobia is all about, the perception of a threat.

Whatever the cause, if there be cause at all, one panic seizure leads the susceptible man or woman to anticipating and dreading another, and another, and another. The pattern is set, the fear deepens, and the range of one's fears is widened. The victim becomes enveloped, swallowed up.

Once you're an agoraphobe, you can't go anywhere. You may never have another panic seizure but you will dread having one. You will dread everything unless you remain "protected" by your shell—your home, apartment or room—in somewhat the way the shell protects the turtle when it draws its head in and hides beneath it. But the turtle is better off because he can stick his head out and go, shell and all. The agoraphobe can't go.

Not just for days or weeks or months. But for years. The literature on phobias tells of agoraphobes who remained housebound for as long as thirty or more years. Extreme cases, these.

Today, with more awareness of the problem and more facilities and techniques available to treat it, the fear-ravaged victim can be helped to recover from the horror-filled existence imposed by agoraphobia.

Mrs. M. is now recovered after being incapacitated by agoraphobia for almost five years. But those years took its toll. She sums it up in a single sentence:

"First I Lost My Job . . .

". . . then I lost my friends, and then I lost my husband."

The strain was too much for her and for those around her.

"I leaned on people," she says. "I had to. Just looking out the window made me feel disoriented. Do you know what was out there? Death.

"That may sound ridiculous to the average person but not to someone who has agoraphobia. I used to feel surrounded at the same time I felt isolated. There were times when my fears were so intense that I'd cringe in a corner and hyperventilate.

"I couldn't even take the medicine they gave me. The pills wouldn't go down. They'd stick in my throat. Spasms in my larynx, the doctor said."

Long before Mrs. M. consulted a doctor, she concealed her growing apprehensiveness with excuses.

"First I lied to myself, then I lied to others to avoid going out."

Childless, nearing age forty when the terror first struck, Mrs. M. worked at a bank as an assistant manager. She had to take a bus to get to work. She couldn't make herself go.

"I was fortunate in that I didn't have to work. My husband made a very good living and was extremely considerate of me. In fact, he had always preferred that I stay home and be an old-fashioned housewife. So when I complained about feeling poorly and wanting to quit, he agreed and said that I should stay home and take things easy."

Neither of them realized at the time that such consideration was misplaced and only served to reinforce the phobia. Unconsciously, Mrs. M. turned her husband's regard for her well-being to her advantage.

"I found myself worrying about him more," she says. "I told him to be careful crossing the street, to watch out for muggers, to eat a healthy lunch. I was becoming as over-protective of him as my parents had been of me."

That may be a clue to the origin of her phobia, according to Dr. Julian M. Herskowitz, Ph.D., director of TERRAP (for *Terr*itorial *Ap*prehensiveness) in New York, a phobia treatment center. "Over-protective parents can project their own fears onto the child," he explains, "and give them the feeling that the world is a dangerous place where anything bad can happen at any time.

"And," he adds, "when a spouse becomes overly concerned about the other partner, that is often an indication that the worry is really about oneself, about being left alone."

So Mrs. M.'s concern about her husband was really topsy-turvy thinking. It was an unconscious cover-up for worry about being separated from her "caretaker," her husband, of being abandoned and unavailable at a time when she might need him most.

In medical terminology this circumstance is known as "pathologic dependency." In ordinary English that means "I need you more than you need me but I can't let you think that."

Mrs. M. became expert at dreaming up excuses to cover up her dread of leaving home. They took in every aspect of day-to-day living and socializing as she recounts a few:

"I'd love to join you for lunch but I woke up with a case of the trots and don't dare leave home."

"You want me to go shopping with you? I wish I could but I'm expecting an important call and can't leave the phone."

"Oh, I've seen that movie. You'll love it. But I don't want to see it twice."

"Canasta tonight? That sounds like fun but why don't you come over here and we'll play at my house. I made some new cookies I'd like you to try."

And so on, and so on, and so on.

"I used to manipulate situations to get friends to come here and keep me company," says Mrs. M. "But after a while they stopped coming."

Some sixth sense told them that they were being used. And then there came a time when Mrs. M.'s husband began to feel the same way.

When he moved out, Mrs. M. prevailed upon her older sister, a widow, to sub-let her apartment a thousand miles away and come live with her for a time. The sister, who was more sophisticated and more knowledgeable, agreed.

"She saved my life," says Mrs. M. "She'd had a friend who was agoraphobic and knew something about this terrible disorder. She became my helper, building my self-confidence while not allowing me to use her as I had used my husband and my friends.

"For the first time in almost five years, I was able to go out the door, taking a step at a time, hanging on to my sister, God bless her."

While agoraphobia, as Mrs. M. discovered, can cripple its victim's life indefinitely unless checked, there are other less complicated but equally vexing and calamitous terrors. In the professional literature these are known as *simple* phobias, not because they are trifling and insignificant, but because they fasten upon a single thing or situation.

Of course, they don't necessarily hold still. They can expand and, like an octopus, reach out to inspire dread of other things and other situations. This will become clear as you read on. What will also become clear in later chapters are the many ways you can keep phobias from expanding and, better still, get rid of them.

But for now let us consider their demoralizing effects on an individual basis.

For starters, here is a list of some familiar simple phobias as they are known diagnostically and by their more common name. Whether referred to by their Greek or Latin designations, or in simple English, they constitute . . .

A Fearsome List

Acrophobia	Fear of height or falling
Aerophobia	Fear of flying

Ailurophobia	Fear of cats
Aquaphobia	Fear of water
Arachnophobia	Fear of spiders
Brontophobia	Fear of thunder
Claustrophobia	Fear of closed spaces
Cynophobia	Fear of dogs
Erotophobia	Fear of sex
Gephyrophobia	Fear of bridges
Hematophobia	Fear of blood
Mysophobia	Fear of dirt or germs
Muriphobia	Fear of mice
Nyctophobia	Fear of the dark
Ophidiophobia	Fear of snakes
Photophobia	Fear of light
Pyrophobia	Fear of fire
Thanatophobia	Fear of death
Triskaidekaphobia	Fear of the number 13
Xenophobia	Fear of strangers
Zoophobia	Fear of animals

To that classic list we should add some new phobias spawned by these high-tech times and contemporary lifestyles. These would include . . .

Cancerphobia	Fear of cancer
Chemophobia	Fear of toxic waste
Criminophobia	Fear of crime
Condophobia	Fear of apartment conversion
Homophobia	Fear of homosexuality
Nucleophobia	Fear of nuclear energy
Obesophobia	Fear of getting fat
Rapeophobia	Fear of rape
Technophobia	Fear of technology
Urbanophobia	Fear of big cities

This list of what may be called neo-phobias may not yet be in common usage but in the view of this author they should and soon will be so included.

You will find them included in this book.

But to better understand the awesome significance of a specific kind of fear, let us consider one of the more common fears, namely . . .

The Fear of Height

Or falling. Greek name: Acrophobia.

Call it what you will. If you suffer from it, you will know what it means to experience terror without mercy. Even when you do nothing more than read a headline about a so-called "human fly," it will freeze your blood, raise your hackles and shatter your nerves.

Consider the case of a man we'll call Harold, now nearing age fifty and afraid of falling since he was graduated from college. His entire way of life has been dictated by his acrophobia.

He lives in a ground floor apartment and works in a store-front insurance agency. He handles only automobile insurance because that doesn't require him to visit clients who might live above the ground floor of an apartment house. His clients visit his office or he meets them at a garage which of course is always located at the ground level.

He loves the theater but cannot attend shows often because of the expense of orchestra seats, and he dare not sit in the balcony or mezzanine.

Not since his college days has he shopped above the main floor of a department store. If he can't find what he wants there, he has to search for a small shop for what he wants.

He has never married and rarely dates because his opportunities are so limited. On the rare occasion that he meets a woman who lives on the ground floor, he invariably finds her not to his taste, or she finds him not to her taste. His sexual appetite is satisfied only by an enormous collection of pornographic magazines stashed away behind more acceptable literature in his bookcase-lined apartment.

Does all this sound funny?

It isn't. Take it from Harold, a melancholy and unhappy man.

"I tried to keep my fear of heights, of falling, to myself," he says, "but it was impossible to do so. Everybody found me out."

What they didn't find out was the intensity of Harold's fear. "They don't really know what I go through" is the way he puts it. "They don't know that just walking past the door of an elevator about to go up makes me tremble. I have to close my eyes to save myself from collapsing and falling down on the floor. I mean, just by looking at the damned elevator door!"

One day, while reading the newspaper, he caught a photograph of a riveter perched high on a beam of a skyscraper under construction.

"I broke into a cold sweat when I saw that picture," he says, "and my insides felt like I was falling down into a bottomless pit. I threw the paper into the wastebasket and took a straight shot of scotch to block that picture out of my mind."

And do you know how it all began?

"I'm not sure," Harold says, "because I've always felt squeamish about heights. But when I came home from college during spring recess, it was a very hot day, and I decided to go up on the roof of the apartment house where my folks lived. The roof was above the sixth floor and I'd parked my car on the street below.

"Well, I was lying there on tar beach, as they say, when I thought I heard someone call my name down below. So I went over to the edge of the roof, behind the fence, and looked down. What I saw was a cop giving me a ticket for parking illegally. He was slipping it under my windshield wiper.

"First I was angry. Then I was frightened. And then, suddenly, I didn't know what I was. I felt sure I was going to topple over the fence and drop down to the street. In fact, I had this crazy urge to jump and land on the cop down there and smash him to the ground.

"Everything went whooey in my head. It seemed to be spinning around my neck. My heart felt like it was going to jump out of my chest. I didn't know what to do. I just crumpled up."

To this day Harold copes by avoiding high places, even places no higher than the top of a long stairway. His entire life is circumscribed by his need to avoid what he perceives as a life-threatening fear.

It is unfortunate that he clings to this way of coping. He doesn't have to. There are many means available to help him conquer his acrophobia. But it's Harold's choice to use only the technique of avoidance. Until and unless he opts for a more effective strategy, like those you'll find in this book, he is doomed to live a very restricted life.

A small degree of apprehensiveness about height is common to everyone. No one understands this better than the producers of motion pictures and television dramas. Show a scene of the hero or heroine clinging to a window ledge high above the street and the audience will eye the scene spellbound, their hearts in their mouths.

Luckily, it's not a feeling that persists. When the scene ends, even if it ends precipitously and tragically, viewers might gasp, but the fear is dissipated.

When we're back in control, we're no longer phobic.

Now here is another common fear to which all of us are susceptible to some small degree. The only absolute exceptions are astronauts, men and women who can and must remain calm and clear-headed within the tight confines of a space capsule. This fear, as you probably guessed, is claustrophobia . . .

The Fear of Closed Spaces

Or, to put it another way, the claustrophobe *needs* space. You will know them by the way they occupy that space.

In the theater, they prefer an aisle seat. Same preference in an airplane, train or bus. At a restaurant, a table that corners them against a wall is a no-no even if it means waiting another half-hour for a "safer" seat. There has to be a place to run, some means of escape. That's why the prospect of taking a cruise can be especially frightening to a claustrophobe. But the right stateroom can eliminate the fear.

The captain of Admiral Cruise's superliner, the S.S. *Emerald Seas,* says many phobics like to try out their sea legs on a three-night weekend cruise from Miami to the Bahamas—not in a small inside lower cabin that increases their feeling of being shut in, but in a bright, roomy, topside stateroom with floor-to-ceiling picture windows that gives them *space*. It's a treat that can become a treatment because being able to cope with their fear of being closed in aboard ship helps them cope with their claustrophobia in other closed spaces as well.

The same happy result could befall anyone who finds a way to manage some aspect of their phobia. Success breeds success.

Unfortunately, until this happens, the claustrophobe must remain alert and fussy, taking great pains to avoid being hemmed in and breaking out in a cold sweat. Such behavior often tends to strike the non-phobic as amusing.

No way.

If you yourself are not a sufferer from claustrophobia, you will understand what it means to be one when you learn of its cruel effects upon one of its victims.

Meet Dorothy. . . .

"I can't stand big cities," she says. "I can't stand narrow streets. I can't stand crowds. I can't stand driving through tunnels. I can't stand anything that closes me in."

Whatever she does, wherever she goes, she is beset by anxiety and lives virtually on the edge of panic. She spends countless hours going out of her way to escape being "trapped," a word she uses frequently.

"I never wait on long lines," she says, "because I feel trapped, especially if the person in front of me is tall and I can't see in front of him. The same thing happens when I drive—always with the window open incidentally—and get stuck behind a truck that blocks my view. I feel trapped, like I'm coming out of my skin, and all I think about is getting out of there before I pass out."

If you ask her what it is, actually, that she is afraid of, she will tell you, "Being locked in, I guess, trapped, with no escape."

Yet she remembers having been "locked in" but once in her life. That was years ago, shortly after she was married. She and her husband were house guests for the weekend at their friends' summer place. During the night, she had to go to the bathroom.

When she was ready to come out, she couldn't. The door was stuck. She leaned against it as hard as she could, twisting the doorknob back and forth, back and forth, again and again, but the door wouldn't open.

"I was frantic," she says. "I was too embarrassed to pound on the door or to yell for help. I mean, I was in the bathroom!"

Ultimately, she had to pound on the door because she had reached a state of panic that was intolerable. She was gripped by a feeling of total terror and admits, "I was so goddamned scared that if I had to come out stark naked waving a roll of toilet paper, I'd have been overjoyed to do it. Just to get the hell out of there."

Yes, indeed, make no mistake about it. "Getting the hell out of there" is what claustrophobia is all about. That simple phrase spells out this "simple" phobia in a nutshell.

What does someone like Dorothy do when she feels trapped?

"The first thing I do is look around for another phobic," she says. "It's not just that misery loves company, as the saying goes. It's that somebody else's misery can be your safety valve. So I look around for somebody anxious, sweaty, agitated, and that's who I head for."

This is how she manages her fear of being trapped in the subway. She says that almost always she is able to spot a fellow claustrophobic.

"You can tell one by the way he, or she, hangs on to the pole or the strap if they're standing, or looks scared to the gills if they've got a seat stuck between two other people. I go right over to them and, I swear, almost every time they can sense a kindred soul. And they're so grateful for my coming by to soothe them I begin to come down off my panicky feeling. And if I can stay calm for just a little while, I know the feeling will pass."

That is the technique she uses to avoid feeling trapped on the subway, a mode of travel that she avails herself of only when she has no other alternative. It's a good stop-gap measure and can be adapted to deal with other simple phobias.

More on that later. Now is an appropriate time to give consideration to another class of crippling fears that go by the name of . . .

Social Phobias

The person victimized by this disabling form of phobic fear is convinced that he is always in the limelight, that all eyes are turned upon him and, therefore, he must take particular care lest he be shamed in company.

In the view of phobia experts, both sexes are equally susceptible. Those who by nature are especially shy or sensitive are especially susceptible.

When in the company of other people, social phobics must be wary of every word they utter, every move they make, every expression they telegraph. Should they do so much as blush when being congratulated, or turn ash-white when displaying nervousness, they will—figuratively—"die of embarrassment."

Fear of humiliation is the keystone of social phobia. Thick-skinned persons are more able to shrug off criticism and even ridicule without being ruffled, or at the very least without showing signs of being ruffled. But thin-skinned persons possess consciences too highly-developed to let such slights roll off them.

They cannot be casual or indifferent. If they can bring themselves to be assertive, they are able to be so only when the need for asserting themselves is absolutely imperative, and they do so at the expense of their fragile nervous system.

Because bashfulness inhibits their ability to form relationships with the opposite sex and a high level of anxiety deters them from dating whomever they may feel attracted to, social phobics have lower marriage rates than all other phobic persons.

Hear now the tale of a bachelor, middle-aged and very frustrated, who shall be named Leo. We call him Leo to point up the contrast between the leonine character suggested by that name—as in "Leo the Lion"—and the kind of pussycat that Leo really is.

We do not do this in jest. In studies of names and their significance in personal development, there is evidence that names can make a difference. Bold names may not lead their owners to develop bold personalities. On the contrary, they may lead to the opposite result. The usual psychological explanation is that because so much is expected, circumstances occur as the individual grows up that reverse the expected result.

The virtues that some parents think go with a name do not necessarily stick to the child. And if they unconsciously raise the child with that expectation in mind, their attitude is likely to do mischief to the child's behavioral development and mold a personality quite opposite to the one they wanted.

Leo had been such a child and never did live up to his name. He was painfully shy. When he had to recite in grade school, he broke out in a rash, and sometimes even wet his pants. In secondary school he could not recite at all because his mind would go blank and he would forget what he was going to say. And every time he broke out in a rash, or wet his pants, or blew his lines, his fear of further embarrassment multiplied.

"I became so fearful of public humiliation," he says, "that I began to do all my socializing on the telephone."

Well, you can do that to a point. That point was overreached when Leo who, mind you, was not agoraphobic, went shopping for one of those stereo carry-abouts that many people like to walk around with, listening to radio broadcasts and cassette recordings through a pocketable stereo headset.

"I found just what I wanted in this high-class department store and gave them my credit card to pay for it," he says. "Nothing in my life prepared me for what happened after that."

What happened was nothing unusual for the average person but was absolutely overwhelming to someone with social phobia. Leo had misplaced his credit card about a week before this incident and had dutifully reported it missing to the credit card company. But some five minutes later he found the card in the pocket of another pair of slacks and re-telephoned the company immediately. He told them that he'd found the card, it wasn't missing after all, and to please not void it.

But of course they did. So when Leo used it to pay for his stereo machine, he was accused of using a stolen credit card.

"If I'd have been accused of murder, I couldn't have felt any worse," he says. "I tried to tell them what happened but it didn't seem to make any difference. The store guard came over and stood there in his uniform looking at me, watching me to see that I didn't run away.

"When I saw that guard, everything seemed to fall apart. I couldn't talk, I couldn't think. I knew I was right and they were wrong but I was so filled with shame that my mind wouldn't do what I wanted it to. I was in a cold sweat, with goose-bumps all over, and shaking like a leaf. It was a horrible, terrifying experience."

Leo's immediate problem was cleared up within a half-hour or less, but his overriding problem became intensified by this experience.

He became fearful of using credit cards, not because he was concerned about being accused again of using a stolen one but because his hand shook uncontrollably when he had to sign for a purchase. The act of signing became for him a humiliating experience. He managed this part of his life only by writing checks at home, cashing them at his bank—after endorsing them at home—and using only cash for buying anything.

Social phobics such as Leo suffer unbelievable indignities when compelled to do anything when other people are present. Some cannot abide the extreme discomfort of dining in a restaurant for fear that they may spill food on the table and suffer deadly embarrassment. And the smarter the restaurant, the keener will be their fear.

The victims of social phobia are poor mixers at parties, if they can bring themselves to attend at all. They do not volunteer to offer an opinion at a family social gathering and, if asked for one, prefer to smile and appear self-effacing rather than make conversation of any kind.

They are put on edge when doing anything in public, from buttoning their coat to shaking hands goodbye. Their extreme sensitivity to "what others think" sets them but a fingertip away from the panic button.

They worry about things that others wouldn't give a hoot about. And the more they worry, the less able they are to draw upon their strengths to cope with their weaknesses. The worry becomes an end in itself.

What is really behind all this worrying?

It is the inability of the real dyed-in-the-wool worrier to dwell in the present. The past and the future are what matter. The worrier ruminates over the past, moons over what was, what has been, what happened before. "Oh, I remember how awful I felt when I forgot the name of my host at the party," he thinks, and that very memory triggers a rebuke by his mind. It deflates his ego and sets up a hierarchy of fears that works like the domino theory, piling anxiety upon anxiety so that he becomes totally distraught.

But the true-blue worrier is also very much concerned about the future. His mind projects the worst. Here come the "what ifs." They pass through his mind on their march to doomsday. "What if I flunk the test? . . . What if the elevator gets stuck between floors? . . . What if my heart stops beating when I'm having sex?"

If the phobic can forget the past and ignore the future, he would stop worrying and no longer be phobic. The healthy attitude is, "What's been has been, what'll be will be." The phobic's attitude is, "You may be right, but I can't depend on it."

The phobic is like the person who denies being superstitious but insists on knocking vigorously on wood to ward off bad luck, explaining, "It's not that I'm superstitious, but why take chances?"

Remember the story about Chicken Little, the feathery phobic who ran about screaming, "The sky is falling, the sky is falling!"? The sky never fell but that didn't eliminate the possibility that it just might fall.

So thinks the phobic, too oppressed by fear to think otherwise. And it is difficult to muster sufficient emotional resources to combat that kind of intense fear. The intensity defines the phobia more precisely and decrees how resourceful one can be in tolerating its effects upon the mind and the body.

What are your most troubling fears? Are there many? Do they paralyze you with worry?

To help you find answers to these questions, and thus make way for finding solutions to the problems they impose, here is a *Worry Chart* that will help you pin down whatever it is that you are most afraid of.

It is a simple quiz based on tested psychiatric principles and deals with things and experiences that may cause fear, nervousness or anxiety.

Essentially, it is a very basic . . .

Fear Inventory

Listed below are 25 common fears. Consider each one carefully. If you consider the object or situation listed *terribly frightening,* place *two check marks* next to it. If you find that object or situation only *somewhat fearful,* give it *one check mark.* And if it *doesn't bother you* at all, do *not* check it.

1) Sharp objects
2) Mice
3) Elevators
4) Flying
5) Crowds
6) Heights
7) Criticism
8) Being alone
9) Meeting strangers
10) Open spaces
11) Falling
12) Riding a bus or train
13) Insects
14) Traveling over bridges
15) Enclosed places
16) Cats
17) Cemeteries
18) Driving
19) People in authority
20) Loud voices
21) Crossing streets
22) Fire
23) Traveling through tunnels

24) The dark
25) Speaking in public

Now add up your check marks. The fewer you made, the less fearful you are. If they total *less than 20*—that's the *total* number of checks adding the ones and twos together—consider yourself appropriately apprehensive with a healthy degree of anxiety to help you protect yourself against possible danger or embarrassment.

But if you scored *higher than 20* checks, you may be more fearful than is good for you.

You would be well-advised to pay *special attention* to those things to which you gave *two checks.* For these suggest areas where your fears may be strong enough and consistent enough to be called phobias. It is likely that they may even prompt a sense of panic when you anticipate having to confront the object or situation that frightens you.

You may, for example, have double-checked number 19 (People in authority) and be so fearful of such persons that just the thought of asking your boss for a raise will terrify you and inspire a mind-storm that leads to panic.

But there are ways to cool it, even when phobic fear reaches epic proportions, and we will give much attention to remedies—including self-help methods—that deal successfully with the problem.

Right now it might be helpful to touch on the folly of simply trying to suppress one's fear and point out instead the value of facing up to that fear.

Nowhere in our Fear Inventory was listed the fear of choking. Still, it is a source of phobic fear to a great many people. In some cases it is related directly to what is being eaten—a fish, say, that is not filleted—while in other cases it is related psychologically to a fear of being suffocated for whatever reason.

Well, researchers have tried many times to convince such persons that their fear of choking is less real than fantasized. They have done this by asking phobics, convinced of their fear of choking, to drink a glass of water and to try as hard as possible to choke when swallowing it.

They tried this experiment three times a day with the same "confirmed" phobics, but not a single one choked! Even more to the point, the more they tried, the less they felt the same degree of choking.

And when all the experiments came to an end, do you know what happened?

The phobic chokers ceased being fearful of choking or suffocating. When they drank their glass of water, it went down smoothly. So did whatever food or fish it was that had made them anxious and fearful.

It is nice to know that such hardened phobics can be helped to get over their crippling fears. But in order to understand how this can come about, it is important to know something more about how such phobias arise in the first place.

Which brings us to the first place. . . .

Chapter 3

Birth of a Phobia

IN CALIFORNIA, midway between San Francisco and Los Angeles, lies a little farming town called Parkfield, population 34. What makes Parkfield very special is its topographical location, almost directly on the infamous San Andreas Fault. This is earthquake territory, and a United States Geological Survey has predicted a major quake in that area sometime in the next few years.

So it should come as no surprise to learn that all 34 residents of Parkfield are severely smitten by *seismophobia* (fear of earthquakes). . . . Right?

Wrong!

You will probably never meet a less phobic bunch of people than the folks who live in Parkfield.

One young woman remembers a quake that struck some miles away in 1983. The shock waves were felt in Parkfield, sending the school's flagpole swaying, bales of hay tumbling from their wagons and even knocking down some of the townsfolk. Nevertheless, while admitting, "I'll probably be scared when the big one hits," she says she isn't worried, and she doesn't look worried or act worried.

Another Parkfield resident experienced the effects of a far stronger quake in southern California in 1966 but remains undaunted by this latest prediction.

"I feel safer living on the fault line in Parkfield than I would if I were working in a high-rise building in Los Angeles," she says.

But perhaps the most unconcerned resident of all is Donalee Thomason who, with an equally unperturbed husband, their son and his family, raise cattle and hay on the family farm.

She says that if she worried about the predicted quake, "I'd be in a padded cell in a hurry!"

Well, what does all this apparent lack of concern among the residents of Parkfield, California, tell us about phobias?

For one thing, it tells us that phobias may be even less predictable than earthquakes. For another thing, it tells us that more goes into the making of a phobia than the real possibility of actual danger.

This should come as no surprise. For we have seen how phobics feel demoralized not by realistic threats to their well-being but merely by their perception of personal peril. No real danger confronts them and yet they feel imperiled.

These perceptions vary as people's personalities vary. What scares one will not at all intimidate another. Moreover, there are many phobics who will boldly face real danger without apprehension while cowering in fear from some insignificant provocation they view as terrifying.

How about the courageous lion-tamer who thinks nothing of taking his life in his hands twice a day to demonstrate his mastery over a cageful of vicious beasts . . . but trembles uncontrollably at the sight of a moth circling about the lamp in his bedroom?

His moth phobia certainly doesn't diminish his bravery in the lions' den but it does make clear a puzzling contradiction in the ways of human behavior.

Quite possibly, while the folks in Parkfield may be able to shrug off any worry about a potential earthquake, some may dread far less consequential events like crossing a perfectly safe little bridge, getting up on the dance floor at a social gathering, or picnicking on the grass (lest an ant cross their plate).

Why might some experience such fears while others escape them entirely? How do phobias come alive and take possession of their victims? What makes a phobic phobic?

Good questions, all of which bring us to a very fundamental proposition which states that . . .

All Phobias Have to Start Somewhere

That somewhere could be anywhere and strike at any What we're talking about is the frightening experience of losing control over one's feelings and the circumstances that contribute to those feelings.

If we can't control whatever it is that we're afraid of, and for whatever reason we're afraid of it, then we're sure as hell going to be hurt. That's the gist of phobic thinking.

When it comes to comprehending the why and wherefore of such thinking, it is helpful to look upon the mind as a kind of master computer. It has hardware—the basic machinery and wiring that was built-in at birth. Call it inheritance. And it has software—the programming developed by one's life experiences from an early age. Call it environment.

So, essentially, you're a somebody for purely genetic reasons. This is the basic you. Your basic temperament was wired in at birth, and it's going to influence the way your nervous system responds to everything that happens to you.

Remember, you are very much an individual. Your brother or sister may respond quite differently to the same kinds of experiences because their basic temperaments differ from yours. If the computer's hardware is different, the software's effects will be different as well.

In other words, the experts feel that there probably is a genetic underpinning to the formation of a phobia in later life, a kind of pre-disposition to becoming phobic to some degree. In fact, it is theorized that everyone may be so pre-disposed, but that doesn't mean that everyone will become phobic.

It is not unlike what happens in the case of cystic fibrosis, diabetes or cancer. "Probably everyone inherits a gene that predisposes you to cancer," says Dr. Jack Gorman, Director of Biological Studies at the New York State Psychiatric Institute, "and if you come into contact with some environmental toxin, the combination of gene and toxin may produce a malignancy."

Then again, it may not. It all depends on how pre-disposed you are to that happening.

Theoretically, all of us may harbor a phobia "germ," but in most of us it will remain dormant because something in our nature keeps it quiescent.

At least, unless and until something takes place to activate the deadly gene-and-toxin combination that, in turn, activates the dormant "gene" and releases a phobic reaction.

A traumatic event can make this happen to a susceptible individual and one of the most traumatic is . . .

An Unexpected Terrible Fright

Few if any personal experiences mix the elements of surprise and violence so grossly as does rape. It is a fearsome psychic as well as physical assault that can shatter the entire structure of emotional, social, moral and biological assumptions that determine a woman's concept of femininity and masculinity.

A study of rape victims by the United States Bureau of Justice concluded that the victims suffered serious traumatic effects for months or even years afterward.

Among the pernicious effects of what has been called the Rape Trauma Syndrome are trembling, sweating, nausea, nightmares, memory loss, depression, loss of appetite, and a persistent fear of darkness, being alone and, often, all sexual activity.

"It is not a groundless fear that women feel," says Pauline Hart, visiting scholar at Harvard Law School and an expert on rape psychology and legislation, "and the fear becomes a means of social control."

In other words, the victim of sexual assault may alter her entire life-style in order to be able to keep a rein on her fear.

She may sleep with a gun under her pillow, carry a knife in her purse or resort to drugs to calm her nerves before attempting to go to sleep.

"Mostly, the trauma of a sexual assault leads to episodes of anxiety," reported Dr. Stefan Pasternack, a psychiatrist at Georgetown University's School of Medicine.

"These could be quite intense and triggered by small everyday incidents like the sudden ringing of the telephone, or the sudden appearance of an unfamiliar man when walking alone.

"Complete social withdrawal is sometimes the way a rape victim deals with her anxieties. Distrust of men could last a lifetime, especially if a woman's first initiation into sexual life comes about via rape. Without a doubt, she is going to be more traumatized."

Those comments sum up, more or less, the transition from fear to phobia. The trauma triggers apprehensiveness and overloads the nervous system to a degree where the fear becomes overwhelming and disproportionate.

It is worthwhile to consider the differences, and similarities, upon two victims of sexual assault, one young and still a virgin, the other approaching middle age and married. First, the young virgin. . . .

Terry's Story

She was sixteen when it happened. She is a pretty girl and dresses fastidiously. But more than a year after the incident, she still speaks in whispers and lowers her eyes in shame in recounting her story.

"I met this boy at a school dance. He was new in town and said he didn't know anybody. We danced and I said he could walk me home.

"Along the way he tried to kiss me. I wouldn't let him. That made him angry. Very angry.

"Before I knew what was happening, he had dragged me off the road, saying he'd kill me if I opened my mouth. He began tearing at my clothes and I pleaded with him, 'Please don't do that, it's wrong, it's wrong.'

"He wouldn't listen to me. He shoved his dirty handkerchief into my mouth and threw himself upon me. I think I must have fainted then because when I opened my eyes, he was gone.

"I was half-naked and something hurt me. I looked down and saw I was bleeding.

"I never dated since that time, and I never will. I hate sex. I hate my body. I wish I could take my breasts off!"

Terry's trauma was compounded by the fact that her trust in the young man had been misplaced, that she had been violated and that her "first time" resulted not from mutual love but from an awesomely terrifying seizure of her body. She had been robbed of both mental and physical control of her personal self.

She has extended her distrust of this man to all men and has become truly phobic about even low-level male-female relationships. But she is not simply afraid of men or sex. She is afraid of almost everything. Her innate sensitivity and emotional immaturity have served to intensify her apprehensiveness.

The trauma of her experience at a vulnerable time of her life set loose that phobic "germ" to which we referred earlier.

This does not mean that her phobic fear is here to stay. Despite the shock, the trauma and the still-present hurt and anger, even such deep-seated emotional time bombs can be made to explode harmlessly and dissipate the phobic fears they engender.

Terry may need help to accomplish this, or she may not. There are many kinds of do-it-yourself approaches to overcoming even deep-seated phobias, as will be demonstrated later in this book.

But here we are dealing with the origins of phobias. We have seen how a frightfully traumatic event can affect a young virginal woman. Now let us examine its effects upon a married woman nearing middle age. . . .

Geraldine's Story

"I used to be a woman who had no fear of anyone or anything. I'd go anywhere, do anything. That was before I was raped. And I had a good rape."

A good rape?

"That means I wasn't hurt. That's all that's good about it, but that's what it's called at rape crisis centers."

It happened when Geraldine's husband was away on a business trip until the following day. It happened in the late afternoon when Geraldine was returning home from her job as interviewer at a personnel agency. She was accosted while unlocking the door to her apartment.

"I hadn't heard him following me—he had sneakers on. He stuck a knife in my back and demanded money. I gave him what I had—about twelve dollars. I thought he'd go but he didn't. 'Get in the bedroom,' he said, pushing me through the door and closing it behind him.

"Until then, I had never thought of rape, only of violence, of being slashed to death. Now he had me alone, all to himself. I was so scared I didn't know what to do except obey.

"I did what he told me automatically. He made me pull down my skirt and told me to take off my underpants. Then he made me put him inside me. That was the most terrible part, having to touch him and insert him.

"My thoughts became all jumbled up. I was suddenly scared of becoming pregnant or getting AIDS."

Fear of AIDS, yes, but fear of pregnancy when you're well over forty?

"I only thought of me as me, a woman, that's all, not as a woman of a certain age. It didn't matter that I was married or that I'd been fucked many times willingly and eagerly before I was married. Those might have been rational thoughts but my mind was not behaving rationally at that moment.

"Being rational then meant my telling him he wasn't using a contraceptive. He didn't even hear me. He was so tense he wanted me to hold him and I just couldn't do it. He slipped out of me while he was ejaculating, all over me.

"Then he ran out, saying, 'Can I come back?'

"My first feeling was shock, numbness. I wanted my husband but I knew I couldn't reach him. I was afraid to call the police but I finally made myself do so.

"They came around pretty quick and wanted me to get into their patrol car to look for the guy. But I just kept crying so they took me to the hospital emergency room.

"It was horrible. Everybody seemed to be looking at me. The doctor who examined me was so cold he disgusted me almost as much as the rapist."

But her ordeal was not yet over.

"Later, the police showed me some mug shots and I identified the rapist. I told the detective I thought I'd seen him in my neighborhood. Well, sure enough, they picked him up a week later.

"Then I had to go to court and answer all kinds of questions like it was me who was on trial. I got the feeling that they couldn't understand how a woman reacts out of fear for her life, that they didn't think I had to give in. Can you imagine that?

"But the guy was convicted and that made me feel better. It also helped that I happen to have a wonderful husband who stood by me all the way. Without his support I think I would have broken down."

So what is the residue of this traumatic experience and the traumatic events that followed it?

"I have phobias. I'm fearful of going out alone at night. My husband must go with me, and I hang on to his arm. Even so, I find myself looking behind me to see if anyone is following us. My husband keeps telling me to look on what happened as just an experience, that life is filled with terrible things and that was one of them.

"He's right. It's the only way to view it. If I'm going to overcome my fears, I have to be realistic. That takes time."

Time is an important factor in overcoming a severe phobic reaction. Ironically, it can also be an important factor in the birth of a phobia.

The point being made here is that while you may be phobic about elevators because you once got stuck in one between floors and it scared the living daylights out of you, that is not the only route to elevator phobia. It might have more to do with your life experience in general than with a one-time experience of being trapped between floors.

You can actually learn to be phobic. All it takes is time, a vulnerable personality and an anxious upbringing. Along with an unrealistic fear of elevators may come unrealistic fears of thunder, lightning, wind, water, you name it.

What we are dealing with here are phobias that result over a period of time as a consequence of . . .

Learned Behavior

Research on panic attacks and phobias suggests that people like to have a tangible excuse for being fearful when actual circumstances do not merit such fear.

"Some do better for having an explanation of why they have the fear," says Dr. Jack Gorman. "It helps them justify their fear."

But that isn't always the case. There may be no contributing trauma, neither a major trauma such as rape nor a relatively minor trauma such as a stuck elevator.

Consider people who, for no reason that they can put their finger on, worry a lot. A Penn State University psychologist, Dr. Thomas Borkovec, thinks that such persons learn to worry.

What he calls "high-worry people" are extremely anxious, often depressed and nearly always expect the worst to happen. Their minds are constantly primed for worrying about almost anything.

"Fear, particularly fear of failure, is the main worry pump," he says. "Self-consciousness, making mistakes, meeting people for the first time, failing tests, criticism, and having to be the leader are components of fear of failure.

"Making mistakes is particularly bothersome, and mistakes are avoided by postponing decisions and anticipating as many negative outcomes as possible. Fear of rejection plagues worriers. Almost any future event threatens them, and ambiguity is their ruler."

Do you remember our reference to the mind as a kind of master computer?

Well, the gist of learned behavior that paves the way to phobia formation is the stuff that is fed into that computer. Parental yearnings, peer ridicule and accidental misfortune all help to program that computer and generate the kind of worry that makes fear of failure a predominant aspect of one's life-style.

In the long term, the phobic effects of such learned behavior can be catastrophic unless the victim is fortunate enough to be able to adapt to circumstances that are less than he or she expected in life. Otherwise, the disappointment can verge on the tragic.

The best way to demonstrate the potentially devastating effects of a phobia that can arise from learned behavior is to cite a case example. Let us head this . . .

The Boy Who Was Taught to Be Phobic

He had a first name but was always called Junior to distinguish him from his father with whom he shared that name. He was bright, tractable and lovable. To the delight of his parents, he talked early, walked early and showed promise of becoming a real somebody when he grew up.

The somebody they expected him to become, and that he himself expected to become, was a doctor, a medical doctor, a rich medical doctor. He had all the mental equipment necessary to meet that goal.

Except for one shortcoming.

He didn't do well on tests. He became nervous whenever he had to take a test. To overcome his nervousness—and raise his marks in school—he cheated. He was an expert at cheating.

He became equally adept at making excuses for not having to take tests. Since his classroom work was spectacular, he often was able to get out of taking a test. He also got help from his mother who sensed his anxiety when Junior was preparing for a big test. She could empathize with him because her own anxiety coincided with his. She worried along with him about the outcome.

Or was it he who worried along with her?

At any rate, Mom sometimes worried so about Junior's nervousness that she misinterpreted his symptoms—hard breathing, cold sweats, trembling hands—as signs of sickliness and reported them as such to his teachers.

Junior was excused. Off the hook. He could take a make-up test some other time. But those times rarely came.

About the only kind of test that Junior was comfortable with was an open-book test. That kind of test spared him the anxiety of having to cheat or worry about failure.

Insecure though he was, Junior made it to college and was graduated near the top of his class. Some called him an overachiever because he had to study day and night to earn top grades. And there were others who called him a cheat because they spied him hiding answer cards at test times in his shoes or cribbing from another student's paper.

The sad part was that he didn't need such crutches. He was very bright, possibly brilliant, but he had been taught—not deliberately—to feel otherwise. Too much was made of his abilities. Too much was expected to materialize from these abilities.

And because he was sensitive and vulnerable, he became a patsy for those who loved him all too dearly and who lavished upon him more anxieties than he could manage. He became a slave of fear.

No, he never did become a doctor. He was too fearful of failing the medical board examination required for entrance to medical school.

He became a carpenter.

The choice was clever. He avoided the need to use his mental skills by electing to use his manual skills which were competent enough.

Avoidance of the thing one fears. That's the watchword of the phobic. Junior learned it early in life and spent years perfecting it to accommodate his growing anxiety and fear of failure.

He met the criteria suggested by phobia specialist Jerilyn Ross, Director of Public Education for the Phobia Society of America, located in Rockville, Maryland—bright, creative, perfectionistic, accustomed to keeping strong feelings to himself as a way of handling stress.

"Then suddenly," she says, "there comes a major change in that person's life where he feels trapped and he feels 'I've got to get out!' Usually, it has to do not with a single incident but with his whole life experience."

Junior's "pièce de résistance" was the need to take the medical board test. That was the challenge that proved too much for him. He felt he had to "get out"—and he did.

That explains the birth of a phobia in behavioral terms. The psychoanalytic view, however, is different. Here, what we have termed the phobia "germ" in order to explain more succinctly the origins of phobias, the "germ" is the product of an unconscious cover-up for what is perceived as sin or wrong-doing.

You can look upon it as a way of coming to grips with guilt feelings by repressing them. Unfortunately, they can pop up in disguised form as a phobia. In other words, you may think you've come to grips with your guilt feelings by repressing them with one part of your mind, but another part of your mind thinks otherwise.

The kind of phobia conceived as a result of this psychic conflict can be aptly described as an . . .

"If It's Taboo, Don't Do" Phobia

It works like this. You do—or merely want to do—something that your moral upbringing says is wrong, forbidden, taboo.

But having done it—or merely wanting to do it—you must suffer the consequence, which is guilt. And this deed, whether real or imagined, is too horrible for you to face. It offends your highly-developed conscience.

So you push it all the way back in your mind to repress it and banish it from your memory. Ah, but those taboo feelings are not so easily gotten rid of. They are still alive and they emerge in different form.

Say, for example, that for one reason or another you despise your father. You hate someone whom you feel you should love. Well, to display such hatred would be intolerable. Besides, you still have a bit of good feeling about him when he shows you a kindness. Moreover, since you live at home with him, you can't avoid him.

How do you resolve the problem?

You don't. Your unconscious mind does it for you. It shifts the hatred from your father to some less demanding object, perhaps a dog your father owns. It's much easier to hate the dog, avoid the dog, and to express fear of the dog—rather than fear of your father.

How did fear come into this?

Very naturally. Your moral upbringing tells you it is wrong to hate your father, so you'd better watch out or you'll be punished for having such feelings. That makes you afraid of him.

Doesn't life become simpler if you're afraid of a dog instead?

Without question. It's a swap that rests a lot easier on your conscience.

Sometimes the route to the birth of an "If it's taboo, don't do" phobia takes several twists and turns before it blossoms into full-grown phobic life.

The case of Jonathan, the name by which he will be known here, is typical. Reared in a highly principled home where virtue, in the best sense, was cherished as the most honorable characteristic of a law-abiding, God-fearing person, the potential for sin and/or wrong-doing always lay just around the corner.

Long before he entered pre-adolescence, Jonathan knew that masturbation was taboo, maybe not for other kids, but for him. Still, he couldn't stay his hand.

This knowledge, plus the fear of discovery, made him quite anxious, as you can imagine. Guilt, fear, and a growing sense of shame worked together synergistically upon his personality. But he endured the increasing anxiety manfully while continuing to enjoy the illicit pleasure of what he viewed as self-abuse.

Then a most unexpected and unpropitious incident occurred while he was in the tub taking a bath. A storm blew up outside and he could hear the rain beating hard against the bathroom window. He felt warm, cozy, snug. He wished he had a naked girl in the tub to screw with. But all he had was a cake of soap and his hands.

Precisely when he reached the moment of ejaculation, a shattering thunderclap frightened him so that he made a great splash, sending bathwater and sperm flying high in the air, against the bathroom wall and on the floor.

With shaking hands, he thrashed about wildly with wash rags and towels to wipe the wall, the floor, and finally the tub itself, being ever so careful that not a single telltale drop of sperm was stuck anywhere to give him away.

He never masturbated again. He didn't abandon his need for sexual gratification but he engaged prostitutes to fill such needs. That way he didn't have to touch himself.

He developed a peculiar habit of washing his hands, over and over again, many times each day. It was an obsessive ritual.

Then came a reluctance to shake hands. With anyone. Or to hold hands. If he could not avoid doing so, he would make every effort to wash his hands in the nearest bathroom or, if that wasn't possible, to at least rinse them off at a drinking fountain or beneath a sink faucet.

From fear of damnation and fear of disease he advanced to fear of authority. Policemen represented such authority and embodied symbols of punishment.

Jonathan arrived at the age of maturity without becoming mature. He never married. He never felt clean. And he never felt safe.

All because he once was a "bad" little boy who played with himself—and enjoyed it. He tried to repress those pleasurable feelings, especially after that thunderbolt hit, but they popped out in an altogether different guise, in feelings of self-disgust.

Now he lives in terror of punishment.

That's why Jonathan experiences feelings of intense fear, heart-thumping palpitations and clammy skin whenever he sees a policeman.

The fear is groundless, of course, but the symptoms are real. He needn't suffer, he can be helped. It's plain simple phobia. Not panic. That's something else.

Which brings us to the purely biochemical factors that can be responsible for the eventual emergence of a phobia. Help is available here, too, but of a different kind.

Here's a phobia whose birthright is a panic attack. First comes the panic attack, then the phobia, nearly always the most crippling phobia of all: agoraphobia. And it has nothing to do with trauma, learned behavior or taboos. That initial panic attack is the result of . . .

A Biochemical Birthing

"Every mental event is a biological event," says Dr. Jack Gorman, who, along with his colleagues Dr. Donald F. Klein and Dr. Michael R. Leibowitz at the New York State Psychiatric Institute, has done numerous studies on the subject with a host of volunteer subjects.

"We are absolutely convinced," he says, "that people get agoraphobia as a consequence of repeated panic attacks, and there is clear genetic evidence that they are so predisposed because of their biological inheritance."

A simple test seems to prove the point. When such persons are given an infusion (a constant flow) of a chemical agent called sodium lactate, they experience many of the symptoms of a panic attack—faintness, rapid heartbeat, sweating, shortness of breath, and so on.

If they are truly "lactate sensitive," they build up to a tremendous crescendo of extreme apprehension. And, as was indicated in the first chapter of this book, women fare worse than men.

The important thing to keep in mind is that not everyone is susceptible. There must be something in your genes, and in your brain, that makes you susceptible.

Furthermore, other studies suggest that some people may be susceptible even to caffeine in large doses to a degree that the panic button could be set off.

Dr. David Sheehan, a noted research psychiatrist at the University of South Florida School of Medicine, has coined the term "anxiety disease" to describe the biochemical basis of panic disorder.

He has pointed out that people who suffer sudden devastating panic attacks while crossing the street, for example, tend to associate the attack with crossing the street.

"But, really, there's no association at all," he says. "It was just an accidental occurrence."

Dr. Gorman adds his own observation. "There are women who will insist that because they had their first panic attack when they had a fight with their husband, that's what provoked it.

"But was this the first fight they ever had? I hardly think so. They probably had many more, but never suffered a panic attack."

Can you deny that logic? If you've been the victim of panic attacks and have blamed their occurrence on a particular incident, think back to how many times similar if not identical incidents presented themselves without causing you to panic.

You may discover that the trigger was biochemical, not situational.

But no matter what the underlying reason may be for a panic attack, it is a terrifying experience. It makes you worry that it will happen again. You become extremely apprehensive. And over a period of time that fear becomes incorporated into your life-style. First you avoid this, then you avoid that, and then you avoid this, that and the other thing. Everything—when you become a confirmed agoraphobe.

That is the vicious cycle of a biochemically induced phobia. The only thing you did to deserve it was being born with an ultra-sensitive brain and nervous system. Your biology did you in.

But don't despair. Your biology can also make possible a permanent cure. No more panic attacks, and no more being chained down as a prisoner of agoraphobia.

How?

That will come later in this book. Now our concern is the birth, not the aborting, of a phobia.

So far we have dealt with what may be called "classic" phobias because they are common to so many people and, despite much new information on their causes and their cures, they continue to plague millions who have not had recourse to such new information.

But contemporary life has spawned phobias that until very recent times were not acknowledged as such. They were dismissed with silence, or as "scare stories" and nothing more.

Then, when the scares began to spread to more and more people, and on every level of society, they became real. As such, they were not phobias.

Never forget that phobias are based on a personal illusion of reality rather than on reality itself. It's the perception of reality that triggers the physical symptoms of fear in phobia reactions.

Now, everywhere, that perception has been heightened because the reporting of the fears on which they are based has broadened to so great a degree. In print, in television and on radio we are sensitized to it over and over again.

We refer here, of course, to what is sure to become the leading phobia of our time . . .

Cancerphobia

"The entire area of cancer is understandably fraught with anxiety, suspicion, and myth," says Dr. Bruce Ames, one of America's foremost cancer scientists, chairman of the biochemistry department at the University of California at Berkeley.

The key word there is "understandably," suggesting clearly that there is indeed good reason to be wary of this life-threatening disease. The problem is that such wariness can go too far and become phobic.

And this is what is happening.

"Cancerphobia is a national phenomenon," says the American Council on Science and Health, "and many Americans, if asked, would probably cite cancer as the cause of death they fear the most."

The seeds of cancerphobia were planted years ago with recurring reports by well-intentioned organizations that issued dire warnings against this, that and the other thing, all of it very good advice indeed.

But along with it comes word of a relative or friend who has succumbed to cancer, or is undergoing the hell of chemotherapy. And along with it comes word of people we admire—actor John Wayne comes immediately to mind—who fought back against cancer and lost. Here the potential phobic thinks more on the loss than on the fact that for many years his or her favorite movie star *won,* successfully prolonging life and the quality of that life despite suffering from cancer.

As we have said before, if you're going to be phobic, you are going to believe the worst. When you read a news report from the World Health Organization that "the overall number of deaths from cancer increased steadily from 1960 to 1980 in the industrialized world despite advances in preventive measures," you are bound to be scared stiff.

If you weren't so scared, you might read on and learn that the increase in cancer can to a great extent be attributed to an increase in longevity. The longer one lives, the more likely it is that one will die of something, even cancer.

You might, if you are prone to be phobic, pick at the bad news and ignore the good news that spells out preventive measures to guard against cancer—no smoking, a change in diet, more frequent medical examinations, and so on.

You are likely to be more influenced by stories in your newspaper concerning people who, apparently, felt misled by their doctors and were diagnosed incorrectly.

There was a news story, for example, that told of a woman who'd been dismissed by doctors as "paranoid" and "cancerphobic" because she continued to complain of feeling lumps in her breasts which they reassured her were harmless. But when she underwent a mastectomy and followed it up with radiation and chemotherapy, she took her case to court and was awarded $1 million as compensation.

Even more to the point, Dan Rather reported on the CBS Evening News that more than 13,000 women underwent "prophylactic mastectomies" in 1984 out of fear of getting breast cancer because their mothers had it . . . even though they knew there was no guarantee that they wouldn't get it anyway.

That's pretty frightening stuff, even for a non-phobic.

And then comes the news, repeated over and over again, analyzed over and over again, and questioned over and over again by respected medical specialists, that the President of the United States had colon cancer.

On the one hand, the news is very good. President Ronald Reagan's surgeon calls a news conference to announce that the patient's chances of living a normal lifespan are "excellent."

But this is followed by an admission that, according to *The New York Times,* "a statistically strong chance also exists that the cancer could recur at any time."

Well, this could confuse even the most non-phobic reader who may be inclined to believe the best, not the worst, but is put off by the suggestion that there are no guarantees that even a robust, powerful individual who has practiced moderation in his day-to-day activities can escape the possibility that malignancy cannot strike elsewhere in his body—no matter how basically healthy he might be or how proficient his medical care-givers.

Let's face it. We're talking about the President of the United

States. If ever cancer was relegated to the back page of our favorite newspaper, it now moved to the front page. And from now on, it will stay there.

Cancerphobia is a generalized response to often conflicting statements about the disease. On one hand, the National Institute of Health issues a bulletin proclaiming: "The news about cancer is getting better all the time."

On the other hand, people start to wonder, "If the President can't escape it, how can I?"

If you're one of these people, and your life has been touched by cancer because someone you love or know has died from it or suffered from it, you may indeed be a candidate for cancerphobia.

But you may have no real reason to feel frightened. You may have the right genes, not the wrong ones. You may be able to profit from having taken appropriate preventive measures. So, if you nevertheless dread cancer with the kind of skin-crawling dread that only phobics know, your problem may be cancerphobia.

Fret not. Cancerphobia is more curable than cancer. More to the point, your fears are probably groundless. This is not to say that you should regard yourself as immune to the risk of ever getting cancer. All of us are at risk to some degree.

There are measures you can take to minimize such risk. Your doctor can advise you on this. Listen to his or her advice and take realistic steps to reduce that risk. This may help to put you back in control of your overriding fear and the irrational extension of that fear to a degree that victimizes you and renders you helpless.

Your capacity to take this advice depends on your personal vulnerability to phobia. How phobia-prone are you? Do you have an unsuspected weakness for becoming phobic? Are you the sort of worry wart who, one way or another, is destined to be phobic?

Here is a Worry Chart to help you answer the question.

What's Your P.Q. (Phobia Quotient)?

Even if you know that you are phobic about something, this little self-test can help you pinpoint those aspects of your mind-set that trigger phobic responses.

Just answer *Yes* or *No* to the following questions. Think before you answer, and be definite about your answer. Do not vacillate or skip questions. Just answer *Yes* or *No*.

1) Do you ever feel like a fraud?
2) Do you worry about saying the "wrong" thing?
3) Do you double-check the door after you've locked it?
4) Do you have to urinate before an important meeting?
5) Did your parents worry about you when you were a child?
6) When things go splendidly, do you knock on wood?
7) Are you a bit of a fusspot and overly neat?
8) Do you have unspoken feelings about being a sinner?
9) Did you ever panic for no apparent reason?
10) Do you shrink from doing things that cause you anxiety?
11) Would you rather walk around a ladder than under it?
12) Are you unexplainably uncomfortable when having sex?
13) Do you worry about passing wind in company?
14) Were you ever trapped in a truly frightening situation?
15) Do you go out of your way to avoid anything or anyone?
16) Has your spouse or a parent expressed disappointment in you?
17) Do you ever freeze and become tongue-tied when put on a spot, perhaps in school or on the job?
18) Are you a moody person?
19) Do you have a close relationship with a phobic person?
20) Are you greatly troubled about the prospect of aging, getting sick, having an accident or going broke?

Add up the *Yesses* to the above questions. Divide the total by 20 (the number of questions) to get your Phobia Quotient. For example, if you had 10 Yesses, you divide 10 by 20, which gives you a Phobia Quotient of 50%.

The lower your P.Q., the less likely that you're phobia-prone. If you scored 25%, that's good. If you scored over 75%, that's not so good.

If you scored in the range between 25% and 75%, you may be anxious to a degree that could—if it hasn't already—give birth to a phobia, given the right circumstances, perhaps a severely traumatic event.

No matter how you scored, you will find it helpful to give a lot of serious thought to your *Yes* answers. They are revealing. They tell you something about yourself, about your true personality, who you really are, and the ways you respond to the world around you.

It is important that you get a handle on yourself, to know your strengths and your weaknesses. And the sooner the better.

Because phobias don't stand still, as the next chapter makes very clear.

Regardless of its origin, the progress of a phobia is inexorable. . . .

Chapter 4

It Gets Worse Before It Gets Better

PHOBIAS ARE RARELY nipped in the bud. Once they take root, they grow like weeds.

Why?

For the most part, because a phobia in its earliest stage is generally not acknowledged as deserving more attention. The initial effect may be minimal. All you have to do is avoid whatever it is that you fear. If you are able to do so without a lot of trouble or discomfort, that almost certainly will be the way you choose to treat the problem.

Some things are easy to treat that way. If, for example, you are terrified of pyramids for one reason or another, it shouldn't be too difficult to avoid them. Just stay out of museums and don't visit Egypt on your next vacation.

However, most things are not so easy to avoid. Take *ailurophobia,* a fear of cats. Avoidance will be far more difficult. Not only are you likely to become apprehensive about a cat crossing your path wherever you go, but you will also cringe with fear if you spot a picture of a cat in a magazine or happen to catch a cat food commercial on your TV set. And should you ever be startled by the sound of a loud meow, you may reach the point of panic.

The more often you meet up with a cat one way or another, the more intense will be your phobic reaction. At every confrontation, your body will be stressed. The wrong kind of hormones will be activated and this can raise havoc with your entire nervous system. Over a period of time, such chemical reactions can elevate severely the degree of your phobia, fanning what was once little more than a spark into a five-alarm blaze.

Dr. Mary F. Asterita, assistant professor of physiology and pharmacology at the Indiana University School of Medicine, says, "If the stress response is experienced over and over and over again, becoming chronic in nature, then these hormonal changes can become detrimental to the body in many ways."

So, clearly, it is unwise to ignore a phobia when it is still in its infancy. While you wait for the phobia to declare itself more worthy of your attention, the phobia takes on a life of its own. It spreads and becomes increasingly crippling. The waiting game always favors the phobia.

Have you ever thought about how many teeth have rotted away because the people whose mouths once held those teeth were afraid to visit a dentist?

According to Dr. Edwin D. Joy, chief of oral and maxillofacial surgery at the Medical College of Georgia, there are 12 million dental phobics in the USA, most of whom fortunately visit a dentist despite their fear.

"But some people," says Dr. Joy, "cannot bring themselves to seek dental care because the fear they carry with them is absolutely paralyzing.

"If anyone manages to calm them down long enough to come into the office, the slightest medical smell of the office can set off a panic reaction. The mere sound, no matter how hushed, of the drill can cause them to turn to jelly. And if they're on the verge of hyperventilating when they enter the waiting room, the sight of the dentist coming at them with a needle can be absolutely devastating, the very end.

"And none have yet experienced even the slightest pain. The dentist had not yet touched them or even asked them to open their mouth. Just the thought, the anticipation, of having dental work triggered a paroxysm of phobic fear."

Men, he says, are more phobic than women because while women will admit they have a low pain threshold, men will not.

They keep their fear inside, their anxiety builds up and they reach a breaking point when their self-control runs out.

So strong is phobic fear, he says, that even third-party payment availability—free dental care—makes no difference. The phobics simply cannot bring themselves to believe that modern dentistry can be pain-free or nearly so.

At the dental phobia clinic in Mount Sinai Hospital, N.Y., Dr. Theodore Goldstein is doing fillings without drilling by using an innovative chemical, "Caridex," to soften decay away. That helps eliminate fear of the drill but not necessarily fear of the dentist.

"Dentophobia is one of the most persistent phobias," says Dr. Joy, "because the mouth is such a psychologically charged area. It takes in air, it takes in food and from our first day of birth it was the area from which we grasped loving warmth from our mother. We use our mouths to express emotion and also for sexual gratification.

"The idea of a dentist poking his or her fingers into this zone of intimacy creates enormous anxiety. Couple this with an uncontrollable fear of pain and you have a very resistant patient."

And, ultimately, rotting teeth, or bleeding gums, and the real pain of having to undergo far more radical dental treatment in order to be healthy and look healthy.

Blame it on the phobia that got away!

Now let's consider an altogether different phobia that got out of hand and picked up momentum rapidly. It started off innocently enough at a shopping mall when Mrs. McKay lost her cool because . . .

She Couldn't Find Her Car in the Parking Lot

"It wasn't the first time I forgot where I parked the damn car," she says, "but those other times I found it fast. This time it was different.

"The lot was huge, and it was on three different levels. I'd been shopping by myself for hours in shops on all three levels and I just lost my bearings.

"What made things worse is that mine was a small car. There were so many bigger cars parked it was like looking for a needle in a haystack."

What happened?

"After I went to each level and looked around, but couldn't find my car, I became very disoriented. I began to get palpitations. I was loaded down with packages but my arms became too weak to hold them. I had to drop them.

"I felt weak all over. My legs were like jelly. I was sure I was either going to faint or drop dead on the spot. Oh, it was so embarrassing!"

She thought she was going to drop dead and she was embarrassed. Sounds illogical, but not to a phobic having a panic attack. Terror and humiliation often go hand in hand at such times.

Well, Mrs. McKay did not die, nor did she faint. A security guard noticed she was in an obvious state of panic and came to her rescue. He picked up her packages, helped her to locate her car and, when she had recovered sufficiently to assure him that she was well enough to drive home, he told her to take it easy and let her drive off.

But that incident marked only the beginning, not the end, of Mrs. McKay's phobic misadventure. The fear of panicking again did not let go.

"That was the last time I went to a shopping mall alone. I would drive only if I had at least one friend along and we wrote down exactly where the car was parked. But even so, I found myself getting anxious every time we went out to find the car."

But she wasn't alone, and she had made a written notation of where the car was parked.

"I know it doesn't make sense," she says. "But when you're afraid like I was, you can't make sense out of something that doesn't make sense. I mean, it all depends on how you look at things. I couldn't see things clearly. I couldn't reason with myself. No matter how safe I was, I didn't feel safe."

Mrs. McKay had to stop driving to shopping malls. In fact, she became too fearful of going to shopping malls no matter who was driving, whether in her car or someone else's. The shopping mall itself had become a place to dread.

"I kept trying to convince myself that what happened before wouldn't happen again," she says, "but the closer we came to the shopping mall, the more I kept feeling, 'It's time to get nervous, we're almost there!'

"And one day I got the point where my fear of panicking was so strong I lost control of myself complete and begged my friend to please turn around and take me home, I felt sick."

She said she felt sick. That was the first of many excuses she would be using to get out of doing things, or going places. It was a legitimate enough excuse inasmuch as she did feel genuinely "sick," but in reality it was more of a cop-out.

"I couldn't go anywhere, I wouldn't go anywhere," she says. "I stopped driving altogether because I was afraid to park anywhere, even in my own driveway!"

Her husband was solicitous of her feelings but was becoming increasingly impatient with her reluctance to leave the house.

"For a while," she says, "I was able to go to parties with him when he drove the car. And I was able to ride a bus if I had to because I wasn't doing the driving, or the parking, and there were lots of other people around so I didn't feel so alone. I was even able to fly on a plane with my husband to see our kids who live a thousand miles away and one of them was sick. I made my husband pull down the shade so I couldn't see outside, so I guess not knowing quite where I was, I wasn't afraid to be there."

Another choice example of phobic "logic."

But by now you can surely sense that Mrs. McKay was well on the way to becoming agoraphobic. And she had travelled many phobic miles away from the parking lot in the three-tier shopping mall to arrive at a destination that she could not leave at all. No way. Home is where she stayed because only there did she feel safe.

There is a happy ending to Mrs. McKay's story. She has recovered from her agoraphobia because her husband did learn, after matters had reached a point where the marriage was strained to the breaking point, that help was indeed available.

In retrospect, it is somewhat amazing to learn how a seemingly trifling unchecked fear can fester and spread to so great a degree.

The impetus for Mrs. McKay's decision to give up her car arose not from a fear of driving it but from a fear of panicking when she couldn't remember where she parked it. In a way, it's like being fined for a standing violation and not a moving violation.

If the latter had proven to be the source of her fear, that would have amounted to something else. And that something else is called . . .

Driving Phobia

It appears to be far more prevalent than even phobia specialists suspected. In a report published in the *American Journal of Psychiatry,* Drs. Juan Roman De La Fuente and Carlos Berlanga Cisneros, of Mexico City, observed, "Driving phobia appears to be an increasingly common psychiatric disorder in the urban setting."

The cause?

Heavy traffic that doesn't move. You want to drive but you can't. You can only wait in bumper-to-bumper traffic and creep along. If you do this day after day with a consequent build-up of stress, that could set off the panic button or produce debilitating symptoms that stop just short of panic.

"We have seen a number of patients with no history of phobic responses or other significant psychopathology," the doctors comment, "who have developed driving phobias after one or more episodes of traffic congestion."

After having been stuck in traffic for anywhere from twenty minutes to several hours, they commenced to experience powerful phobic symptoms including sweating, palpitations and a fear of losing control because of the intense mix of anger and impotence.

"One of our patients," said the doctors, "had to move to a smaller town because he could no longer function in the city."

Well, that's one way of beating it before it beats you. But not everyone is able to pick up and move so easily.

It is an open secret that many motorists deal with the anxiety build-up of driving phobia by holding in their feelings until they reach home and only then do they get relief—when they race to the bar and mix themselves a double highball or dry martini.

If that happens often enough, they can stop worrying about being phobic and begin worrying about being alcoholic.

Before making an alcoholic adjustment to deal with a phobic reaction, it might be wiser to check out the car and make mechanical adjustments that may make driving, in or out of traffic, more comfortable. See that the motor runs smoothly, quietly, and the cooling system functions properly to alleviate any fear of the engine over-heating when traffic is stalled. Check out the interior comfort level, the seat, the safety belt fit, and the stereo.

Doctors everywhere are becoming more concerned about the increase in driving phobia because of the increase in urbanization. Streets within cities are more crowded with cars, and roads that lead in and out of cities are also more crowded with motorists who commute to and from work.

The effects of difficult driving situations—in congested traffic and on freeways—were demonstrated clearly in a research study on the fear of driving in Houston, Texas.

Dr. Roy J. Mathew, a psychiatrist at the Vanderbilt School of Medicine in Nashville, Tennessee, headed a team of experts from there and from the Texas Research Institute of Mental Sciences in Houston. The study was launched when the doctors discovered that patients were breaking appointments at the clinic with increasing frequency.

What reason did they give?

They were afraid of driving there!

A major newspaper published the story and the telephones at the clinic began to ring with calls from people who suffered from the same fear of driving. Those selected for the study admitted to feeling anxious while driving under normal conditions in the city, felt their fear was inappropriate and excessive, and were concerned that it was interfering seriously with their lives.

And what did they discover about the men and women who participated?

They discovered that the fear of driving reached phobic intensity only when these motorists were trapped in traffic or frightened to death on the freeway. Yet, even at such times, the subjects agreed that their anxiety was "out of proportion to the demands of the situation, but their fears could not be alleviated by reasoning and explanations."

What was the doctors' conclusion?

"Their fear of driving was beyond their conscious control, and it caused them to avoid the fear-evoking situation," they said.

And they concluded that such reactions justified calling their problem a phobia which they took care to define as "a special form of fear that is out of proportion to the demands of the situation, cannot be explained or reasoned away, is beyond voluntary control, and leads to avoidance of the fear situation."

When they couldn't avoid the need to drive, they tried to reduce their anxiety level by turning up the music on their car radio, singing aloud, smoking, doing some relaxation technique, or gulping down a tranquilizer (a very dangerous strategy).

We'll be dealing with these and many other kinds of coping strategies for all sorts of phobias in a later chapter. For unless one has some tricks up his or her sleeve to cope with the phobia or feared panic attack, things will surely worsen.

Either you stop a phobia in its tracks or it stops you. It might stop you just for a time, or it might stop you for good. And it could begin early, very early, in your life as a . . .

Childhood Phobia

Many years ago there was a popular song entitled "The Bogeyman Will Get You If You Don't Watch Out." And some parents, grandparents, uncles, aunts, other siblings and even schoolteachers used to invoke fear of the bogeyman in a small child to make him be "good."

That sort of thinking is now passé, and good riddance to it. But a little boy or girl still has plenty of things to be afraid of with no help from anyone, and despite reassurance from authority figures that there is nothing to be afraid of.

It is not uncommon for children, especially between the ages of two and four, to experience intense fear of the dark. Some have to be put to sleep while a night-light is left burning to allay the fear. And a particularly anxious child might be awakened during the night by a frightening nightmare.

Even when accompanied by other fear-provoking stimuli such as thunder, lightning or scary TV cartoons, these childhood fears rarely develop into full-grown phobias. For a while they may become worse but eventually they will just fade away along with other childhood memories.

Less likely to fade away, however, is a fear of animals, a catch-all category that includes everything from dogs to birds to insects. Such fears can be transmitted from parent to child. A mother who displays evident phobic fear about mice, for example, could unconsciously send a subliminal message to a sensitive child and arouse that same fear.

On the other hand, the fear can emanate from a scary experience with the animal itself—a dog bite, say—that leaves a kind of emotional scar on the child's nervous system. And no less an authority than Sigmund Freud has written that childhood phobias can get their start merely from "picture books and fairy stories." Today he would probably include pictures—moving pictures, no less—on the TV screen.

Animal phobia in children is unique in that it may appear to vanish with childhood but may, in fact, simply remain dormant and emerge many years later in adulthood. As Dr. Robert L. DuPont pointed out in a classic paper in *The Journal of Pediatrics*, "Only animal phobias in adults are typically the residual of childhood phobias," and added the explanation that "animal phobias virtually never begin after childhood."

So it may be that the moth you fear today may be traced back to the fuzzy caterpillar that, for some reason, frightened you in childhood.

While it is not possible to be absolutely certain about the connection between animal phobia in childhood and a most peculiar but very devastating phobia that manifests itself in some elderly people, it is not at all unlikely that such suspicions are correct.

The phobia in question is called *acarophobia,* defined as a morbid dread of animal parasites, insects or mites. It is being brought to the attention of dermatologists with increasing frequency.

"I'm seeing many patients of both sexes, most of them elderly, but not all, who suffer from this phobia," says Dr. Joseph A. Penner, a prominent New York dermatologist.

"They are absolutely convinced that they are being eaten up by insects even though such fear is totally unwarranted," he says.

"They produce scraps of dead skin, tiny scabs that probably came from scratching and even bits of debris from their clothing. This is how they try to prove that their fear of infestation by insects is real.

"No matter how carefully I examine them, no matter how patiently I reason with them, they remain unswayed from their belief. And they go from one specialist to another in hopes of finding someone who'll agree with them. They may sound crazy but they aren't. They're phobic."

The cure, of course, doesn't lie with the dermatologists, but with phobia specialists or with some practical self-help techniques, as we shall see.

Childhood phobias are best treated by allowing kids to express their fears openly and not be ridiculed or punished for doing so.

Dr. DuPont stresses that "it is almost always best to help a child get back promptly into the fear-producing situation rather than let the avoidance behavior continue," because facing the fear "is typically less distressing than the anticipation" of exposing himself or herself to the object of the fear.

In other words, when a child falls off his bicycle, for example, encourage him to get right back on it. That bit of common-sense treatment can nip the phobia in the bud.

If a child displays school phobia, the same thinking is applicable. It could mean the difference between the development of a crippling phobia and the maturation of the child into a healthy, functioning adult.

Most psychiatrists agree that school phobia arises from the child's anxiety about leaving the parents. He has to be reassured that nothing will happen to them or to him while he is away.

"Tell the child that you know he feels bad, but that he must go to school," advises Dr. Rachel Gittelman, a professor of clinical psychology at Columbia University College of Physicians and Surgeons.

"Encourage him to try it. And once you've talked it out, don't dwell on it endlessly. That will only make him feel defeated."

There are situations and circumstances that would leave a grown-up unscathed but be destructive to a young, impressionable child. This is likely to happen when a sensitive youngster has to deal with . . .

Sickness in the Family

Lucille thinks she was about four years old when her mother had pneumonia. She remembers hearing her coughing and hearing whispers about her spitting up blood. She also remembers climbing out of bed one night and peeking into her mother's room and seeing a tent over her head, not realizing that her mother was being given oxygen to help her breathe.

"I was so frightened I ran back to my bed and pulled the covers over my head," she says. "I didn't tell my father or anyone what I'd seen or how scared I was. I tried to make believe I'd only dreamed it."

But that was only wishful thinking. It was no dream. It was real. What wasn't real was her understanding—or, rather, lack of understanding—of that fear.

"I really didn't know what was happening to my mother," she says. "All I knew was that something was different. And I think that's what I was afraid of."

Quite right. That is how Lucille's phobia was implanted in her young mind. It was reinforced again and again because, as she recalls, "My mother always seemed to be sick. And I wasn't the kind of kid who'd pour out her feelings to anybody or cry or anything like that. I kept things in. I don't know why, but I did. That was me."

When Lucille was seven years old, her mother was taken to the hospital and underwent surgery for a hysterectomy. All that

Lucille was told was that her mom was sick but that she'd be okay again after staying in the hospital for a while. Her father and other relatives used explanations such as this to reassure her.

Through no fault of their own, they didn't understand how the mother's sudden absence and her recurrent illnesses could accumulate in a heap of nervous anxiety when the focus of these fearsome circumstances is a close-mouthed super-sensitive little girl.

Then they compounded the problem and its effects by sneaking Lucille into the hospital to visit her mother, thinking that such a visit would be reassuring. Of course, the effect was just the opposite.

"She was lying there like she was dead," says Lucille. "This I distinctly remember. I looked at her there in the bed in this strange room, and I knew it wasn't her room because there was somebody else lying in another bed in the same room surrounded by people crying. And I wanted to kiss my mother but before I could do so, I fainted!"

Actually fainted, at least so she remembers it. Perhaps she only felt that she was going to faint, because a panic attack—and that's what it was—leads up to the point of fainting but rarely if ever reaches that point.

However, at the age of seven and with a solid phobic background, the sights, sounds and smells of a hospital could be enough to convince the young victim that she had indeed fainted.

Lucille's mother recovered. Lucille didn't. Her phobic fear became fixed. From that traumatic moment on, she became unable to ever visit anyone in a hospital.

"Everything about hospitals set me off to palpitating, feeling faint and going bananas," she says. "The sight of the place, the institutional set-up, the antiseptic smell of the halls, the wheelchairs, the gurneys, the nurses, the whole ambience. I had to visit a close friend once in a hospital and I tried to do it. I told myself, 'You've done this before, you can do it again.' But I couldn't. I was just talking to myself. I just couldn't make it."

As Lucille grew up, her apprehensiveness about sickness increased. In looking back on her childhood, she says, "It seemed reasonable to me that as a small child I should have been frightened to see my mother so sick, and to become fearful that she would die. Worse yet, there was nothing I could do to forestall her dying. Isn't it reasonable to believe this?"

Yes, but as we have already noted, the true roots of that fear were not based on reality but only on the child's perception of reality. Moreover, it is certainly not reasonable for a grown young woman to go on feeling such apprehension about doctors and hospitals. She knows, in fact, that her fears are irrational but is unable to control them.

When her own husband became ill and had to be hospitalized for a relatively minor problem, she could hardly bring herself to visit him.

"It was hell for me to go there," she says, "but I forced myself to go. I owed it to him. I had to go. But I expected to pass out at any minute."

She didn't pass out. And she herself managed to enter a hospital to give birth to her first child. She offers some insight into the mind of a phobic when she explains, "I was able to because that was me, not somebody else. I went to the hospital for me, to have my child."

But her unwarranted fear of hospitals did not go away. Nor did her fear of doctors. Nor did her fear of sickness. As a matter of fact, Lucille to this very day suffers from all these fears and, most particularly, from *cancerphobia*.

That is the phobia to which she has displaced all her anxieties, apprehensions and dread. The phobia triggered in early childhood has been transformed and magnified, which only goes to show how persistent a childhood phobia can be.

The concern she expressed for herself when forced to enter a hospital to give birth apparently raised fears about self-preservation. The specter of cancer, which we have already dealt with, became a kind of magnet for her new-found preoccupation with herself. It was just a skip and jump away for a mind prepared for this kind of progression from early childhood.

She is now finally learning how to come to grips with her phobic fears. We will deal with the many techniques available for doing so in the chapters that follow.

If there is any area in the phobic scheme of things where the apparent basis for the fear becomes worse before—if ever—it gets better, that has to be the sexual area.

It all boils down to boy meets girl, boy loses girl, boy gets girl, and oh-my-goodness . . .

Boy Can't Make It With Girl

There is no sense in quoting statistics on this matter because statistics change as the times change, and the times indeed are changing.

Some self-styled experts say that the younger generation is over-sexed. Other self-styled experts say that the younger generation is under-sexed, too busy making money to make honey, and furthermore the modern young man on the move is suffering from competition with the liberated young woman on the move—even when the two of them are married.

In the latter case, *erotophobia,* the fear of sex could be a way of compensating for a deep dislike of the opposite sex. After all, who wants to sleep with the competition?

But other considerations must be taken into account. Whatever one's notions about maleness and femaleness might be, the male must still deliver the goods. The problem arises when he can't.

Furthermore, the problem becomes magnified by the extensive publicity accorded to sexual prowess in the media. It isn't hard to conceive that many males who, actually quite virile, might feel diminished in comparison with the gung-ho macho types depicted in the movies, on TV or in the magazines.

Fear of failure is aroused and, as Dr. Viktor E. Frankl, the world-famous psychotherapist has noted in his book, *The Unheard Cry for Meaning,* "Fear always tends to bring about precisely that which is feared."

So sexual impotence indubitably increases with the fear of failure. Dr. Frankl says, "Whenever potency and orgasm are made a target of *in*tention, they are also made a target of *at*tention.

"Attention is *withdrawn* from the *partner* and whatever the partner has to offer in terms of stimuli that might arouse the patient sexually. As a consequence, potency and orgasm are in fact diminished."

The male, convinced by futile tries that he is impotent, avoids sex altogether and, says Dr. Frankl, "A phobia really starts when this pathogenic pattern of avoidance has been established."

There are many techniques for dealing with this sort of phobia and overcoming it, whether it be based on hostility towards the partner or a catch-up of guilt from years of believing that sex is dirty and wrong.

We will later discuss such techniques because this is the kind of phobia that can really snowball if not treated early. It *always* gets worse before it gets better.

And as pressure on both sexes increase to heighten orgastic pleasure and frequency, this phobia is likely to increase as well.

Still, even the simplest phobia, one founded on pure superstition, can worsen until it becomes debilitating and crippling.

And what is the essence of pure superstition?

The number 13, that's what, and few would dispute that. Well, let's have a look at what happens to someone who suffers from . . .

Triskaidekaphobia . . . What's That Again?

If you're superstitious, so be it. But be aware that this weakness could make you more amenable to becoming phobic. That has been pretty well established in previous chapters.

All right, so here is a brief tale of a man who admits to being superstitious, particularly about the number 13. He doesn't know why, except to believe that 13 has always been referred to as an unlucky number and he goes along with that belief.

Well, there has to be more to it than that if his fear of the number 13 is truly of phobic proportions, but that is of no concern to us here. We don't want to know where it came from, but only where it is going, or has gone.

It certainly has gone and taken its toll. This man—he's real but we're not going to bother naming him because we're not going to go into any real detail about him—*thinks* that he began to become fearful of the number 13 when he became 13 years old.

This sounds ridiculous and probably is. What is more likely is the fact that he was raised in a superstitious family that carefully took note of every black cat, every ladder on the street they walked and every happening that could be considered an "omen."

Regardless of the cause, this man became incapacitated by his 13 phobia, to an extent that is hard to imagine. Among other things . . .

He refused to get out of bed on the 13th day of the month . . .

He always skipped page 13 of his newspaper, magazine or any book that he was reading . . .

He would not get off at the 13th floor of any building even if his job depended on it . . .

He moved from the state of Massachusetts when he discovered that there were 13 letters in its name . . .

He paid an extra penny or an extra dollar on any bill that totalled 13 cents or 13 dollars . . .

He divorced his wife on the 13th anniversary of their marriage, then re-married her, and she understood. . . .

There is no need to go on. In time, one superstition led to another and the fear of the number 13 expanded to take in other fears. Given the intensity of the original fear, the new fears multiplied and the cumulative degree of phobic fear rose and kept rising.

Phobic fear that is fed by superstition often leads to *thanatophobia,* an extreme dread of death and dying. Terry Kuraner, known in New York City and Florida as "Mr. Monument" because of his reputation as a monument salesman, has witnessed how this phobia affects some people far more than grief itself.

"I've seen close members of the deceased," he says, "too terrified to set foot in a funeral home, go to the cemetery or attend a wake or an unveiling. Even people only remotely related to the deceased or the bereaved refuse to leave their car. Some of them break out in cold sweats and even pass out like they are having heart attacks.

"And I found that these extreme responses have nothing to do with their feeling grieved over the death. They just are scared stiff of coming face-to-face with dying. Because they recover fast and are perfectly okay once they're on their way from the scene. My wife says they have a phobia and I think she's right. I'm glad I don't have one or I'd be out of business."

His wife *is* right. The problem isn't grief, it's phobia. No matter whether it's triskaidekaphobia, thanatophobia, or whatever, these phobics can help themselves if they really want to. And so can you, no matter what your phobia or how seriously it affects you.

It all boils down to how much you can take. Professional phobic experts have laid out a way of pinpointing the degree of phobic fear from 1-to-10 so that the phobic sufferer can have some means of identifying the degree of anxiety with which he or she greets this or that object or situation.

If you're a 1, that means you're calm as can be; if you're a 10, that means you're experiencing sheer terror. By setting 10 as a peak level, a maximum emotional response to a dreaded situation, you as a phobic will know that you have reached the limits of your fear. You know that you've reached the top, that you can't go any further, and that you aren't going to die or go crazy after all.

It is very important for you to know—and be convinced of this—if you are phobic. Because just knowing this will give you reassurance and help you stem the progress of your phobic fear.

With that in mind, give your attention to the following *Worry Chart* to help you assess . . .

Your Dread Degree

Here is where you can size up your response to the thing you fear, from Absolute Calm to Utter Terror. In numerical terms, that's equivalent to going from 1 to 10.

This is a very simple self-quiz. Just remember, you are making judgments about your *inner* feelings and not about what is happening around you. Try to overlook whatever it is that you hear, see, taste or otherwise experience from outside yourself. Concentrate instead on the symptoms that claim your body and your mind when you are confronted by the thing or situation that scares the life out of you.

All right, zoom in on whatever it is that makes you unreasonably fearful. Now, keeping that firmly in mind, rate the *degree* of fear you feel when and if you must unavoidably confront that feared object or situation. Imagine the very *worst* that could happen and then check off the number that best describes the degree of your response to it.

1) Calm as can be.
2) A little bit jittery.
3) Uncomfortably uneasy.
4) Decidedly uneasy.
5) Jittery but still in control.
6) Heart pounding and sweaty.
7) A feeling of losing control.
8) Unable to think straight.
9) On the edge of panic.
10) Unbearable sheer terror.

If you didn't check off a number above 5, consider yourself still in command. But if you checked off a number above 5, it's your phobia that's in command.

Stop worrying. Help is only a page away . . .

PART TWO

HOW YOU CAN TAKE CONTROL
(The Solutions)

Chapter 5

You Can Help Yourself

IT SHOULD BE CLEAR by now that worrying about where your next phobic scare or panic attack is going to come from will only increase the likelihood of its happening. But knowing how to intercept it can stop it from happening.

There are dozens of simple strategies you can use to reduce your fear, anxiety or apprehensiveness to manageable proportions.

Our concern in this chapter is not with permanent cures. Our concern here is to spell out easy-to-use stop-gap measures that can de-fuse or limit a phobic attack.

Just by doing that much enables you to deal with the terror of a phobic object or situation. Instead of having to avoid the feared object or situation, you become able to avoid the fear of facing it.

That is a big step for anyone who is phobic.

So if you happen to be approaching a bridge you fear to cross, or to board a plane you fear flying, or to deal with a job interview you dread, here are the *Quick-Fix Strategies* that you can use to abort those fears.

You will find them invaluable if a phobia has worked its way into the nooks and crannies of your life-style and is paralyzing your ability to live a life of joy and fulfillment.

Some of these strategies work better than others at different times, in different places and for different people. But all of them do indeed work.

You must choose the ones that work best for you. You may find that if one doesn't work as quickly as you expected, another one will. You will also notice that some can be applied more unobtrusively than others.

This latter is important. If you anticipate a phobic attack when you're at home alone, any kind of fear-busting technique can be used. But if that phobic attack becomes threatening in a public place, you will naturally want to use only an unobtrusive tactic to squelch the attack.

Quick-Fix Strategies

Essentially, all these phobic "band-aids" are distraction techniques. They are aimed at taking your attention away from the threatening object or situation, and snapping you out of a panic response.

It is important for you to become familiar with all of them and trying them out on yourself—at the first inkling of a phobic symptom—so that you can concentrate on practicing those you find to be the most effective.

Regard them as *power* strategies that put you in command of your phobia instead of vice-versa. You're going to break the spell of your fear reaction by exercising some mental gymnastics.

You are going to get a lot of help from all five senses—touch, sight, smell, taste and hearing. Plus a few more that include an inner sense that involves feeling, and a muscular sense that involves a keen awareness of muscle tension.

Pick and choose what you will and you'll have a veritable arsenal of fear-fighting weapons at your disposal. Don't look for theories as to why this or that approach works for you. Sometimes they'll work for reasons other than those given here as they're described.

If it works, use it!

At the first sign of a phobic symptom, you must psych yourself to make your move against it by calling on a Quick-Fix Strategy for help.

Let us deal first with the sense of . . .

Touch

The mere feel of something familiar can create for you a kind of comfort zone that acts to shield you from fear. The feel of something unfamiliar but unthreatening can serve to snap your mind back to reality.

Try these to short-circuit phobic anxiety . . .

1) *Touch of your own hand.*

You can reassure yourself that you're going to be all right simply by touching firmly one hand with the other, or touching your arm, your cheek, your forehead. This can and should be done inconspicuously to heighten the sensation of secret pleasure.

Remember how President John F. Kennedy used to keep his hands in his jacket pockets when he spoke casually? Perhaps that was his comfort zone, his "safe place."

2) *Wiggle your toes with your shoes on.*

Keep doing this until the fear passes—and it will pass. It's an ideal Quick-Fix for situations where you feel trapped but must act unobtrusively, as in a dentist chair, a classroom or under the dryer in the beauty parlor.

3) *Snap a rubber band encircling your wrist.*

"When you begin to have scare thoughts," says Dr. Julian Herskowitz of TERRAP, "this is a great way to break the chain of phobic thinking and snap back to reality."

By snapping the rubber band smartly against the soft inside part of your wrist, you are using a distraction technique that snaps you back, literally, to the here-and-now.

4) *Swat the back of your neck hard and fast 10 times.*

Obviously, this is something you don't do in front of anybody else, but it can be a lifesaver when you're on the verge of panicking.

Use the palm of your hand against the nape of your neck. Don't fuss around before you do it. Make your move quickly. The deliberate nature of your action helps to make it more effective as a panic-stopper.

5) *Chew on something.*

It needn't be gum. It could be the end of a pen or pencil, an eyeglass stem or a swizzle stick. Some phobics always keep a swizzle stick on them for emergencies.

You'll find this technique more appropriate and more effective than the time-honored anti-anxiety tactic on which it is based—nail-biting, of course.

6) *Click your tongue against the roof of your mouth.*

A nice inconspicuous way of draining off tension and controlling fear—but do it with your mouth closed. As Dr. Edwin Joy, the dentist quoted earlier, said, "The mouth is a very private place."

What you do there with your tongue is nobody's business but your own. This puts you one up on whatever is outside that frightens you. It's your safe place, just like JFK's pockets.

Now let's move on to the sense of . . .

Sight

"Watch your step," your phobia warns you when you come to a bridge you fear to cross.

But are you truly fearful that the bridge will collapse under your weight—or could it be that your real fear is that you will give in to an inexplicable urge to jump off?

Or could it be that the bridge is merely a symbol, that you're fearful of what lies on the other side—that is, might it not be the connection between your present position and where you are going, where you dread going? To your doctor's office for a crucial test? To the IRS office for a tax audit? To your mother-in-law's house?

Whatever may be the meaning of that bridge, don't look across it transfixed. Fix your stare elsewhere. By changing your visual focus you can change your perception of the thing you fear.

Here are some Quick-Fixes that use your sense of sight . . .

1) *Keep an eye on something real.*

You are driving—over a bridge, through a tunnel, on a highway, makes no difference—when you are suddenly seized by an impending feeling of doom.

Perhaps you're getting nervous keeping up with the flow of traffic. Or perhaps you are behind a big truck that looms up in front of you like a wall and makes you feel claustrophobic.

Don't become transfixed by that blank wall. Don't become mesmerized by the traffic whizzing by. Set your sights on something real to restore your mental balance.

Notice the license plate of the truck. Don't try to read it. Just notice it. Then shift your gaze for a quick look at your side-view mirror, then your rear-view mirror. Steal a fast look at your speedometer.

In short, jolt yourself out of your premonition of impending doom by distracting yourself from your phobia—but not from your driving. You don't have to take your eye off the road to deal with reality. On the contrary, you have to impose a perception of reality upon your hypnotic fear.

2) *Watch the seconds fly by.*

This gambit can detach you from fast-building anxiety at a tense business meeting. Surreptitiously, divert your gaze from the threatening figures around you to your wristwatch.

Follow the second hand in its circular chase around the dial. Watching the watch will distract you from feeling that you're being watched.

3) *Change the lighting.*

The amount of light that enters your eye can change the perception that enters your mind. Sometimes, simply dimming the lights or drawing the blinds will prove soothing and promote the feeling that you're in a safe place.

Sometimes, quite the other way, brightening the room will chase the shadow of approaching disaster that is threatening to come over you. Changing the light's color helps too.

Don't you notice how your inner perceptions change in a movie theater when the screen you're looking at goes from dazzling colors to washed-out blahs, and vice-versa. You can alter your perceptions in similar fashion with the Quick-Fix change of lighting described.

Next we take on the sense of . . .

Smell

If you've ever seen a TV commercial for a deodorant, you know that the pitch is for "protection." Of course the real thrust of that advertised message is a promise of protection against personal embarrassment from having an offensive odor.

But smells, good and bad, can have psychological effects as well. The anesthetic smell of a hospital, for example, can trigger unhappy memories of a traumatic illness and stir up old fears. Good smells can do the opposite and have a positive effect on your psyche.

In North Carolina's Duke University, medical psychologist Susan Schiffman is researching emotional responses to odors and has found that the smell of rich chocolate can lift the spirits of depressed patients.

At the John B. Pierce Foundation Laboratory at Yale University, researchers are doing scientific studies on the human sense of smell and Dr. William Cain says, "It's not crazy to think that smell would be one of the sensory stimuli to reduce stress."

In fact, Dr. Gary E. Schwartz, a Yale professor of psychology and psychiatry, is studying the effectiveness of "aroma therapy" on a host of psychic symptoms including phobia. He compared a group of people exposed to pleasant fragrances like that of fresh apples to a group not so exposed and asked both questions designed to elicit signs of stress.

The group exposed to pleasant fragrance showed less stress than the other group, and the degree of stress was measured by blood pressure, heart rate and muscle tension readings.

You can make practical use of such research findings in helping to ward off or cut short a phobic attack. A pleasant smell can do it. So can a shocking one. See if one of these won't do the trick for you . . .

1) *Sniff a hankie.*

Just as a bad smell can trigger a phobic response, a good smell can stop one abruptly. Every woman has a favorite scent, every man a favorite after-shave.

Apply that happiness-evoking fragrance on a hanky, a scarf, or even a shirt cuff if need be. At the first indication of a phobic attack, quickly put that item to your nose and inhale. You will feel comforted.

2) *Let your nose turn you on.*

It's an inescapable fact of life that what one person perceives as an offensive odor another perceives as an olfactory turn-on. And if you're turned on, your phobia is going to be turned off.

So make your own personal choice of the smells that send you up. Don't worry if they seem bizarre. Use them in private to stave off the terror of a panic attack.

The smell of an old slipper, a sweaty shirt, or soiled drawers may turn off a lot of folks. But maybe not you. Keep those objects of your affection handy and bury your nose in them when panic threatens.

3) *Carry a menthol inhaler.*

You can get one at any drug store. Choose the one that stings your nasal passages when you take a deep whiff. That sting can shock you out of a phobic response.

It's a way of snapping back to reality through your sense of smell. It isn't the particular fragrance that makes it work but the sharpness of it on the sensitive lining of your nose.

Moreover, it's handy to carry on your person and can be used unobtrusively, or almost unobtrusively.

4) *Snap back with ammonia.*

This is the big brother of the inhaler. It's a throw-back to smelling salts and spirits of ammonia. Just keep a bottle of household ammonia handy at home for an emergency whiff when you need it. You can even pour some into a small perfume vial and carry it on your person. Take one sniff, no more!

Next on our list of Quick-Fixes is the sense of . . .

Taste

Our taste buds affect not only the way we feel about certain foods but also about the way we feel—period! The oft-repeated statement, "You are what you eat," suggests that your dietary intake reveals something about your personality.

In short, what you eat travels not only to your stomach but also to your brain. The effect on your brain, your nervous system, your mental state, is greatly enhanced by the taste of what you put in your mouth.

And there is something more. Along with the taste comes the feel of the food, the mush or crunch of it, whether it's hot or cold, and whether it's solid or liquid. All these elements are included in this list of tasty tips to knock down your fear . . .

1) *Use a power bite.*

There are few sensations more satisfying to your taste buds than the crunch that comes when you bite down hard on some tasty morsel so that it seems to explode in a burst of flavor. This sort of taste-explosion can blast away your sense of fear.

What you choose to crunch down on is up to you and your taste buds. It could be anything from nuts to mints to carrots. If you expect to encounter a phobic situation, be sure to take along some of these crunchy foods.

When the time comes for you to decide to avoid or face up to your fear, face up to it. Let yourself do so by popping one of your crunchies into your mouth and chomping down hard.

Just one word of caution: be sure your teeth can withstand the crunch.

2) *Chew a fresh stick of gum.*

Here you combine taste with the act of doing something—chewing—to control your anxiety and shortcut a strong rush of fear.

This is not unlike the "power bite" Quick-Fix but is easier on the teeth. But don't depend on a stick of gum to work wonders forever. As the taste goes, so goes the effect it works on your mind.

Get yourself a fresh stick of gum!

3) *Eat some comfort food.*

This is an ideal solution for the social phobic who cringes at the prospect of eating in a restaurant for fear of being embarrassed. Quite without reason, of course, but not if you're phobic.

Order a meal that is easy to eat, not messy and that can be served quickly—for the longer you wait, the higher will go your level of fear and you might try to drink it away with cocktail after cocktail.

Order foods that make you feel good. Perhaps they remind you of your childhood, of being mothered instead of feeling smothered. These might include chicken soup, mashed potatoes, chopped steak and, generally, foods that are on the mushy side and warming to the palate.

The choice is up to you.

You can use this same Quick-Fix at home. Many agoraphobes or persons only inches away from becoming agoraphobes pull down their fear level by serving themselves a plate of comfort food.

4) *Lick a lolly.*

Yes, this is a symbolic way of becoming a carefree child again. But science has added something more to what appears to be no more than a symbolic activity.

Research scientists at the Massachusetts Institute of Technology found that some people have an unconscious biochemical need for a pick-up. And a sweet—like a lollipop—can change brain chemistry fast.

Essentially, though, it's your sweet tooth that can help to take your mind off your phobic apprehension.

5) *Pick yourself up with a pickle.*

Here's the reverse side of the sweet tooth tactic. An ice-cold very sour pickle will make your taste buds sizzle and your mouth pucker.

It is a first-rate way to distract your attention away from "what if" worries going on in your head. Just be sure the pickle is really sour, ice-cold and crunchy!

The last of the traditional five senses is the sense of . . .

Hearing

Musical therapy is an accepted treatment technique for various kinds of emotional disorders. It has psychological validity because music has the power to move people deeply. Its effects reach the brain through the ear.

Confucious, the legendary Chinese philosopher, said that music "makes pretense or deception impossible." If that be so—and there is reason to believe so—it performs this valuable feat by revealing reality to the listener. This is precisely the kind of help needed to fend off a phobic fear.

By becoming able to snap back to reality, to this moment in time and to what is actually going on at this moment in time, phobic fears are at best dissipated and, at worst, at least relieved.

But there is more than music that meets the ear when you use your sense of hearing as a fear-buster. Here are some ways to do it . . .

1) *Turn up the volume when you listen to music.*

Just listening to your favorite music isn't enough to break the back of a phobic attack. You have to listen to it played loud—no matter whether it's a pop tune, a symphony or a rock-'n'-roll favorite.

Don't let it play on and on. But if you're at home or driving in your car, turn the volume way up for a second or two the moment you feel apprehensive. A single loud blast can sidetrack your fear.

2) *Plug your ears with stereo phones.*

This is the portable version of the previous Quick-Fix. Sure, you can use stereo phones at home with your hifi—and that's an excellent substitute for raising the volume in your loudspeakers. Also, by enclosing yourself with a set of comfortable stereo phones, you eliminate all extraneous sound.

The effect on the delicate nerves in your ears is psychological as well. You become preoccupied only with the sound you want to hear. This tends to shut you off from phobic concerns.

You can carry this effect with you by means of a portable stereo device that uses a radio or a cassette. It can help you get safely through an anxious ride on the subway or an equally anxious ride in an elevator.

It serves a similar purpose on airplanes where plug-in phones are provided at every seat. Fearful fliers often plug them in before they fasten their seat belts.

3) *Play an instrument, any instrument.*

You don't have to take music lessons or learn to play recognizable tunes. It is merely the sound and the fact that you are producing it that makes it work.

If you own a piano, pound on the keys. If you have a horn, toot it. If you have a drum, beat it. If you haven't any instrument, buy a harmonica, a kazoo or a tambourine. Anything will do.

When your phobia causes you to feel jumpy, make a noise on that instrument. Yes, this tactic does have a little bit in common with the medicine man's practice of chasing away the evil spirits by banging a drum.

Well, what's wrong with that as a practical analogy? Doesn't phobic terror wear the face of an evil spirit? Be your own medicine man and shoo it off!

4) *Give a little whistle.*

It's a time-honored technique for dealing with anxiety. And it still works. But, of course, you have to be able to whistle. Not everyone can.

If you can't, use another Quick-Fix. But if you can, just the sound of whistling will divert your attention from heart-pounding fear.

5) *Listen to yourself.*

This is a way of putting yourself back in control when your blood starts racing and you anticipate the worst. You will need an inexpensive tape recorder and a blank cassette.

Put the cassette in the tape recorder, pick up the microphone and start giving orders to yourself. This is how you prepare a tape of your voice giving orders to yourself.

In a clear, strong voice—you must do this when you're at ease, not under stress—speak into the microphone and say: "Stop! There is nothing to worry about. (INSERT YOUR FIRST NAME)—are you listening? This is me talking to you. We are the same person. I'm not afraid, so you don't have to be afraid, either. If you don't think I'm real, pinch yourself. See? Now play this tape over again and again until all the fear is drained out of you!"

When you give orders to yourself, you become your own taskmaster, so it's you telling you what to do in order to feel better. When you hear your own voice coming back to you, in a strong self-confident tone, it can lift your self-esteem and prepare you to go out and slay the dragon.

The dragon, of course, is phobic fear. Play the tape before you have scheduled yourself to do something or go somewhere that arouses the dragon.

You will find yourself thinking, "I don't like it, but I can bear it."

When you make use of your senses as power strategies, you effect a change in sensation or perception, perhaps in both. Now we go beyond the traditional five senses for Quick-Fix aids based on what we'll call . . .

Your Muscle Sense

Phobia specialists have observed that muscular stress and anxiety go hand-in-hand. As for cause-and-effect, it can work both ways. When stress originates in the muscles, the anxiety level goes up. When anxieties originate in the mind, muscle stress goes up.

It's not unlike the classic chicken-and-the-egg puzzle. Experts disagree on which comes first.

This can be an advantage to a person with phobia because it offers a double-barreled approach to controlling the phobia. You can attack through the mind or through the muscles. Here we'll use the muscle sense to defuse phobic terror . . .

1) *Let your jaw sag.*

Stress often resides in the hinges of your jaw. When you open your mouth just by letting your jaw drop, you relieve some of that stress.

You can accentuate this de-stressing technique by placing the fingers of each hand on the jaw hinges just below your ears and massaging these areas lightly. Don't rub your fingers against your skin. Simply rotate them in little circles so that the skin moves with them.

Remember to keep your jaw loose when you're doing this. The effect is synergistic. One action helps the other.

This Quick-Fix can bring a sense of calm when you experience phobic fear. It is not a very conspicuous technique. You can use it in a restaurant while pretending to read the menu. It's an ideal way to reduce a bewildering but frightening sense of panic that might strike when you feel uncomfortable in a theater.

2) *Shake your wrists.*

Do this 20 times. Let your hands hang limp and shake. Count to yourself as you do so. The counting adds a distraction technique to an un-tensing technique.

You can get a similar effect by holding your wrists under cold water and letting the water pour over the inner more sensitive sides of your wrists.

Wrist-shaking is more convenient. It's a good tactic to try before making a public appearance at a party, meeting or whatever that triggers stage-fright anxiety.

3) *Use your fists.*

No, not to punch anyone, but to use as tools for tensing and un-tensing stressed muscles that are sending anxious signals to your brain.

Make a fist, un-make a fist. Make a fist, un-make a fist. Use both hands simultaneously. Do this 10 times. And do it hard—real tight, real loose, real tight, real loose.

This tensing, un-tensing, sequence can disrupt those anxious signals going to your brain and help restore a sense of balance to your mind state. It can make a phobic fear go poof!

4) *Try a make-believe chew.*

This is recommended especially to social phobics who fear becoming tongue-tied at the prospect of making a speech. But it can be equally helpful to anyone who suffers phobic fears when having to make a telephone call.

Toby Katz, president of The Speaker's Corner Communications Consulting Group, Inc., in New York City, thought it up and described it this way in *The New York Times:* "This simple exercise consists of 'chewing' a large, imaginary piece of gum, first on one side of the mouth, then on the other, then with the front teeth (you must 'chew' with your mouth open).

"It takes only 45-60 seconds and makes it much easier for the articulators (the teeth, tongue and lips) to function."

Not only does this strategy ease the muscle tension around the mouth, it also works as a distraction from apprehensiveness about speaking up.

Our final set of Quick-Fix aids makes use of your inner sense, your psyche help you make fast beneficial . . .

Mental Flip-Flops

When your mind perceives danger where no true danger exists, you can switch off this false perception by using your mind to alter that.

You can do a mental flip-flop that will help cue you back to reality. And here are some ways to do it . . .

1) *Memorize a shopping list.*

That's the first step. The next step is to keep repeating that list over and over by reciting it to yourself. It needn't be long but it should be somewhat complicated.

Don't merely say: "Butter, eggs, bread, milk, cheese, meat, fruit." Spell out the details: "Half a pound of sweet butter, a dozen eggs, one small loaf of whole wheat bread, a quart of milk, half a pound of swiss cheese, a pound of chopped sirloin, three ripe bananas and two pounds of macintosh apples."

Difficult to remember all that, isn't it?

You bet it is. That's what makes it work. Your mind becomes so preoccupied with memorizing that list that it has no room left for other worries.

When that happens, you alter your perception and the phobic fear it breeds.

2) *Count backwards from the number fifty.*

This is another way of unclogging a mind filled with false perceptions. You have to think hard to count backwards.

If this is too easy because you happen to be a whiz at arithmetic, make it tougher. Count backwards from fifty, or from a hundred, subtracting three each time. It would go: "50–47–44 . . ." and so on.

3) *Recite the alphabet in a special way.*

Here is another variation, this time using letters instead of numbers. Reciting the alphabet in a special way means skipping every other letter: "A–C–E . . ." and so on.

You're taxing your mind with a mental task in the here-and-now that pushes aside disturbing thoughts. Mental gymnastics of this kind can cut off impending fears of disaster.

This and the other techniques work better when you are able to speak them aloud because then they also affect your hearing sense. But when this is not possible because you're in a public place, a silent recitation that visualizes numbers, letters and items in your head can be effective in lowering, if not completely dispelling, your feelings of anxiety.

4) *Do a crossword or other puzzle.*

When your thoughts run in many different directions and you begin thinking about a dozen things at the same time, you tend to lose your mental center of gravity.

You're bound to become overwhelmed and this can aggravate any phobic tendencies. There's no anchor to hold your mind-set in place. This can set the stage for a high level of anxiety or even a panic attack.

What you need is something to bind your anxieties. That something has to have a clearly defined form where everything has its place, like a neat kitchen with every utensil put back where it belongs, or like a clutter-free desk where every piece of paper has been slipped into its proper file.

Word puzzles, most especially crossword puzzles, have this kind of orderly form. In a crossword there is a single space for each letter and for only that letter. As you work on it, you begin to put things together where they belong.

Your thoughts stop running wild because your concentration is on putting things into place. By establishing a sense of order, you help re-establish control of your mental state.

Keep this Quick-Fix in mind, and keep a crossword puzzle in your pocket or purse, the next time you ride in a bus, a plane or subway. It can even help you cope with the terror of a subway being stalled in a tunnel.

5) *Think "Who cares!"*

This is a form of auto-suggestion. It's a way of shrugging off the fear of embarrassment triggered by a generally inconsequential something you did, said or simply thought.

The more sensitive you are, the more likely you are to suffer from this affliction. If you allow your feelings to go unchecked, your fear of embarrassment is sure to worsen.

Instead of thinking yourself into it, try to talk yourself out of it by thinking hard, "Who cares!"

This will help you shrug it off mentally. At the same time, actually shrug your shoulders as you think, "Who cares!" to emphasize that thought.

6) *Imagine your head is hollow.*

This is more than simply thinking happy thoughts. It's having a place to put them.

If you can imagine that your head is hollow, you can go on to imagining yourself filling it full of happy thoughts. Depending on your own particular notion of happiness, your imaginings could include mind pictures of blissful scenery, barrels of money or erotic pleasantries.

This could put an end to doomsday thoughts. And since it's all going on in your head, you can use this gambit anywhere. Nobody will notice.

7) *Say a prayer.*

So simple, yet it works if you're of a religious bent. When you feel disconcerted enough to anticipate fainting or otherwise going to pieces, interrupt those feelings by interposing a little prayer between them and your screaming need to regain your presence of mind.

One young woman with a flying phobia who must fly to keep her job says this is the only means by which she can cope with her fear: "I pray, from the minute I sit down until the plane is up and flying. Then, from the minute I hear the announcement that it's starting to land, I pray again until it finally lands."

She's okay once the plane is in the air but not when it's taking off or landing. Those are the moments when she calls on her Quick-Fix prayer to manage her fear. She uses it selectively. So can you.

And if you don't know any prayers, carry a little prayer book with you. Reading can add to the distraction benefits of your plea to a Higher Being.

8) *Pull your left ear three times.*

If you're superstitious, this seemingly silly tactic won't seem silly at all to you. Use it as a way of warding off frightening thoughts and the physical symptoms they arouse.

Is it magic?

Yes. That's why it works for superstitious folks.

Knock wood!

9) *Rub a rabbit's foot.*

Or an amulet of any kind. It could be a "lucky" penny you've carried in your pocket or purse for years. Or a treasured little heirloom that fulfills the same "lucky" purpose.

You may not even have to rub it, but simply touch it for reassurance. Just knowing it's on you isn't enough. You do have to make contact to make it work for you.

And of course you have to believe in its magical powers. If you do so believe, then you have at your disposal a Quick-Fix to cope with all sorts of phobic apprehensiveness.

These Mental Flip-Flops, together with all the other Quick-Fix Strategies in this chapter, can help stop the progression of phobic fear before it reaches unbearable intensity and perhaps leads the way to the crippling degree of agoraphobia.

Remember, if you're a "10" in phobia terminology, you're in trouble. For at Level 10, you've reached the ultimate in phobic terror.

That need never happen. There's a lot more help ahead if simple strategies are not enough.

The next chapter spells it out. . . .

Chapter 6

A Calming Influence

ONE OF THE SUREST WAYS to shield yourself from the devastating effects of a phobic attack is to learn the art of relaxation. This could eliminate the need to resort to a Quick-Fix Strategy because a well-timed appropriate relaxation response can preempt the phobia.

"You can't be anxious if you're relaxed," says Dr. Donald F. Klein, Director of Psychiatric Research at the New York State Psychiatric Institute.

If you find yourself beginning to tense up when you contemplate exposing yourself to an object or situation that you're afraid of, let your watchword be: "Cool it!"

Easier said then done?

Not really. There are lots of ways to "cool it." And the beautiful thing about it is that you don't necessarily need help from anyone. *You can do it all by yourself.* In fact, a do-it-yourself approach could be the best approach of all because it affords you tangible proof that you can not only confront your fear but can actually *control* your fear.

Dr. Martin E. P. Seligman, a University of Pennsylvania psychologist, refers to such a sense of calm in his book *Helplessness* as "self-produced controllability . . . relaxation that an individual produces himself."

No pills, no potions, no supervisors. Just you, knowing what to do.

Just as your mind can conjure up panicky thoughts that frighten you, it can be trained to conjure up peaceful thoughts that shoo fear away.

Here is a little experiment that can demonstrate to you the power of your mind. It was devised by Dr. Erik Peper and Dr. Andrea Schmid of the Center for Interdisciplinary Science at San Francisco State University to show how mind power can help athletes perform better.

You will need a friend to assist you in doing this experiment. Both of you stand up, facing each other. Now reach out your hand, arm extended, and place your hand—palm up—on your friend's shoulder.

Ask your friend to try to bend your arm at the elbow joint while you offer resistance. Carefully note your degree of resistance and the degree of difficulty your friend requires to bend your arm.

Now repeat the experiment—with one big change. Before you ask your friend to try to bend your arm, close your eyes and concentrate hard, very hard, at envisioning your arm as a strong steel rod extending way, way beyond your hand, for miles and miles. Then, when you have achieved this concentrated mental image, ask your friend to bend your arm.

Note how much greater is your resistance, and how much more force your friend must exert to bend your arm!

Just as your mind can help you control muscle tension, so too can the way you breathe. Do it properly and you will feel relaxed. Do it incorrectly and you will experience some of the symptoms of a panic attack because you won't be getting enough oxygen into your lungs.

When that occurs, your muscles tend to produce sodium lactate, the chemical that precipitates a panic attack in many people. But see for yourself . . .

Take the Breath Test

Sit down. Allow your hands to droop to your sides. Snap your fingers, one hand at a time, about once a second. With each snap, shift your eyes in the direction of the snap.

In other words, when you snap the fingers on your right hand, shift your eyes to your extreme right. When you snap the fingers on your left hand, shift your eyes to your extreme left.

Do this fast, every second, and repeat it at least ten times, more if you can stand it.

Because you will begin to gasp for breath—just as you might do when you have a panic attack!

This happens because, essentially, you have lost control of your breathing and are probably holding your breath as you snap and look, snap and look, over and over again.

Along with a lack of oxygen, chances are that you'll find your heart is beating faster as well. And if you could check your blood pressure, you might discover that it also rose.

When you take in oxygen, you dispel anxiety. You relax. You thus become able to confront your fear.

Breathing exercises can be very helpful aids to relaxation. Some may be more suited to you than others so here are several to choose from. All are based on the same principle but offer different ways to go about achieving the same effect. In any case, the first thing you have to know is . . .

How to Breathe Correctly

A specialist in biofeedback (more on that later), Howard Kay, teaches patients at his Biofeedback Developmental Center in Forest Hills, New York, how to distinguish correct and incorrect breathing habits.

"Place one hand on your chest, the other on your abdomen," he says. "Now breathe slowly, in and out, in and out.

"If you're breathing properly, the hand on your chest should remain stationary. But the hand on your abdomen should rise up and down with every breath you take."

Try it for yourself.

Try it while seated. Try it while lying down.

If you still have difficulty, use the power of your mind to help you concentrate. To do this . . .

Make a Balloon

Not a real balloon. An imaginary balloon. Imagine that balloon is in your tummy and that you're going to blow it up and let the air out by turns.

But wait, there's more. You must imagine further that a straight tube leads from your throat to that balloon. It is a clear tube with nothing in it to interfere with the flow of air through it and with plenty of room for that air to flow through.

Now sit down in a comfortable chair, not slouching, but comfortably seated. Close your eyes. Place your hands as before, one on your chest, the other on your abdomen.

Take a long, deep breath through your nose, very slowly so that you can almost feel it going down that tube and filling that balloon. Your chest should remain stationary and your tummy should rise as that balloon inflates.

Then, deflate that balloon by exhaling very slowly through your mouth this time. Again, you should almost be able to feel the air coming up the tube as you feel that balloon in your tummy deflate.

Take your time doing this breathing exercise. Don't rush it or you'll begin to pant which will completely negate its usefulness. If you do it slowly, deliberately, taking your time between breaths, you will find it to be a very relaxing exercise.

Keep practicing it until you have it right, and until you can do it naturally without the need to employ visual imagery as a helping aid.

A breathing exercise can be a marvelous calming influence when used before confronting something you're afraid of—making a telephone call, meeting your date, going for a drive, whatever. It could be especially helpful in agoraphobia by extinguishing, or at least reducing, the initial sense of approaching panic should it become urgent for the agoraphobic sufferer to leave home.

To make breathing exercises even more effective, you can focus your attention on a healing word as you do them. By adding what is really a form of auto-suggestion to your breathing exercise, you add the convincer that helps make it work and enables you to . . .

Breathe Out Fear

Yes, literally and figuratively. What you're going to ask yourself to do here is to add certain persuasive words to your breathing exercise. The combination produces a near-hypnotic state that intensifies the relaxation effect.

As you do your breathing exercise—slowly, deliberately, repetitively—whisper to yourself the word "Courage!" every time you inhale, and the word "Fear!" every time you exhale.

You breathe in courage, you breathe out fear!

It is so simple a technique you might think it ludicrous. But if you go about it seriously and with every intention that you want it to work, it can indeed work.

Here are two variations on the same technique, using different words. One of these might suit you better than the one just explained.

Again, place yourself in a comfortable position. Take a deep breath, hold it in for a few seconds, then let it out slowly.

But this time, with every breath you take in and every breath you let out, think of just a single word: *Calm!*

"Calm" in, "calm" out, "calm" in, "calm" out, and so on for about twenty seconds. Avoid all distractions by keeping your eyes closed. If, when you open your eyes at the conclusion of this exercise, you do not feel fully relaxed, repeat the sequence.

Now for the second variation. This is especially appropriate for the person who possesses a good sense of humor, for it might actually elicit a laugh. And few things are more relaxing than a good laugh.

Once again, make yourself comfortable. Close your eyes. Take a deep breath, hold it, then let it out slowly.

But this time, you must make two changes in the procedure. First, every time you breathe in, clench your fists tightly. Every time you breathe out, unclench them.

Second, every time you breathe out and unclench your fists, whisper a loud "*Ha*!" Keep clenching and unclenching while you breathe, and keep whispering "Ha" with every exhalation—until you find yourself beginning to smile or perhaps even laughing!

If this technique works for you, that's how you'll know it.

While strategic words can enhance a breathing exercise, words alone can be effective when used as the basis of a meditation technique. Dr. Ilan Kutz and a team of research scientists in the Behavioral Medicine Division of Boston's Beth Israel Hospital found that relaxation could be achieved "by restricting attention to a single repetitive stimulus . . . and if your mind wanders, just re-focus your attention on the word."

Instead of being linked to breathing, the success of this approach is linked to . . .

A Secret Word

It's secret because you selected it and only you know what it is. But it mustn't be a word that holds any emotional significance for you. It should be meaningless, even made up, a nonsense word such as "skootch," "whup" and "bink," just to give you an idea of what a meaningless word might be. And, note, they are all only one syllable, because one syllable seems easiest to concentrate on.

Not for everyone, though. Some prefer to use a phrase, a rhymed couplet, or what is called a "mantra" in T.M. (Transcendental Meditation) parlance.

Like T.M., like yoga, the meditation route to deep relaxation rests on your ability to shut everything else out of your mind except that secret word. You must focus your total attention upon it, and keep repeating that word to yourself over and over again.

You must be very comfortably situated when you start this exercise. Seated or standing makes no difference as long as you are really comfortable.

The light should be dim, your eyes closed, and before you project the word onto your mind or say it aloud to yourself, try to envision the most peaceful scene that you can imagine. Allow it to fill your mind, or more precisely, your mind's eye. It could be a mental picture of fleecy clouds, a gently rippling stream, a sunny meadow filled with dandelions, anything that you find peaceful and reassuring.

Now, gradually allow a mental picture of that word to impose itself, spelled out, over that lovely scene as you commence to say the word softly, but aloud, to yourself. Concentrate on that word. Keep repeating it, over and over, until it consumes your whole attention. When this occurs, your mind will be blank, empty, void of everything except the repetitive resonance of that word.

After a time, perhaps 10 or 15 minutes, you will become transfixed, perhaps even to imagining yourself in what has been called a fourth state of consciousness that is neither sleep, dreaming or wakefulness. You will have entered into a state of deep relaxation, but from which you can emerge whenever you like simply by ceasing to repeat your magic word and so allowing yourself to be distracted.

But you will emerge with a clearer perception of reality in place of the false perception that characterizes phobic fear.

Just don't expect to arrive at this level of relaxation on your first try. This technique, like most others, requires practice, practice, practice. If you find this one particularly to your liking, you should set aside two 15-minute periods a day to practice it.

A good time for the first session would be after breakfast before you start your day. A good time for the second session would be after dinner before you begin whatever activities you have planned for the evening.

Of course, even if you have not mastered the technique fully, you should certainly give it a try any time you feel confronted by a phobic object or situation to lower your anxiety level. You will be calm, but not becalmed. In other words, you aren't likely to be frozen by phobic fear although you may not feel as laid-back as you would like. But at least you are likely to feel comfortable enough to get on with whatever you wish to do.

However, if you find it difficult to master the degree of concentration necessary to make this relaxation method work for you, you might find a faster route to relaxation via . . .

The Metronome Way

You will need a metronome. It could be inexpensive, but it should have a clear, strong, regular beat when wound up and flagged into motion. And it should be able to be set fairly accurately to beat time. If it's a bit off, that's okay. It needn't be precise, but it should be consistent from beat to beat.

Dr. Joseph Wolpe, the noted psychiatrist and pioneer in behavioral therapy, devised this relaxation technique at Temple University, Philadelphia. Here is how you can adapt it for home use when you experience irrational fear.

Set the pendulum to swing back and forth at a slow rate—60 beats a minute. That done, dim the lights or draw the blinds. Now take a comfortable seat with the metronome placed beside you on a table.

Start the metronome by releasing the pendulum.

With each beat, say the following to yourself, one syllable at a time: "Re—lax . . . Let—go . . . Re—lax . . . Let—go . . ." and so on.

Keep time with the beat of the metronome—a single syllable to every beat. The regular, repetitive nature of this exercise—steady, no highs, no lows—will have a soothing effect.

Continue the exercise for 15 minutes.

After you've practiced this technique several times, you will not need to use words at all. You'll need only the metronome. The gentle ticking alone will help you relax, and will do so in less time.

And once you're relaxed, the prospect of confronting your fear should no longer terrify you. For you will have shaken off enough anxiety to enable you to come to grips with your fear and make it manageable.

Relaxation training, no matter what the method, provides a reliable means of re-establishing a sense of control over your phobia. But no one method suits everyone equally. Personalities differ, even among people who suffer from the same phobia.

This is why you must be presented with a choice of relaxation exercises so that you can try them all, then pick the one that works most effectively, quickly and consistently for you.

Here is one that is very popular with Family Physicians, specialists in treating the whole person and certified in that specialty by the American Board of Family Practice.

It can produce profound muscle relaxation throughout the body which, in turn, induces a calming effect upon the mind, and for this reason is named . . .

The Total Body Response

This is a ten-step exercise. It requires time and effort. You can do it in any private place, at home or in the office. However, if you belong to a health club, you might find an agreeable spot to do it there.

It is not designed for emergency situations. Its aim is to help you establish—by repeated practice—an overall feeling of relaxation that may reduce your susceptibility to phobic fears, and perhaps pave the way to permanent cure.

Before you begin, be sure the clothing you're wearing hangs loosely, comfortably, on you. No binding, no tightness. Easy clothes. Or stark naked if that's your preference and there is no danger of embarrassment.

Bear in mind that you are not to leap from one step to another without pausing. *You must pause for 20 seconds between steps and rest!* If you're ready to begin, lie down.

Now here are the ten steps to achieving Total Body Response . . .

1) Close your eyes and do a deep-breathing exercise. Choose any such exercise from those described previously.

Repeat the exercise 5 times.

REST FOR 20 SECONDS, KEEPING YOUR EYES CLOSED.

2) Squeeze your right fist and bend your right arm up and tight to your shoulder to tense the muscles. Then open your fist and lower your arm to relax them.

Repeat 3 times.

REST FOR 20 SECONDS, KEEPING YOUR EYES CLOSED.

3) Squeeze your left fist and bend your left arm up and tight to your shoulder to tense the muscles. Then open your fist and lower your arm to relax them.

Repeat 3 times.

REST FOR 20 SECONDS, KEEPING YOUR EYES CLOSED.

4) Tense your lower face and upper neck by spreading your lips wide to tighten your jaw muscles. Then let go so they ease back to normal.

Repeat 3 times.

REST FOR 20 SECONDS, KEEPING YOUR EYES CLOSED.

5) Tense the upper part of your face by frowning hard. Hold it for a few seconds, then let go and relax.

Repeat 3 times.

REST FOR 20 SECONDS, KEEPING YOUR EYES CLOSED.

6) Hunch your shoulders up into your neck, hard as you can. Then let go.

Repeat 3 times.

REST FOR 20 SECONDS, KEEPING YOUR EYES CLOSED.

7) Tighten your chest and abdomen. Squeeze in hard. Then relax.

Repeat 3 times.

REST FOR 20 SECONDS, KEEPING YOUR EYES CLOSED.

8) Push your right leg forward and point the toe out as far as you can. Feel your leg muscles tighten. Then let your leg and toe relax.

Repeat 3 times.

REST FOR 20 SECONDS, KEEPING YOUR EYES CLOSED.

9) Push your left leg forward and point the toe out as far as you can. Feel your leg muscles tighten. Then let your leg and toe relax.

Repeat 3 times.

REST FOR 20 SECONDS, KEEPING YOUR EYES CLOSED.

10) Tense up your whole body, condensing all the previous steps into one and tightening both fists, both arms, your face and neck, chest and abdomen, and both legs.

Hold that overall tension for 10 seconds.

Then let go and relax.

REMAIN WHERE YOU ARE, EYES OPEN NOW, AND ENJOY THE FEELING OF TOTAL BODY RELAXATION FOR AS LONG AS YOU LIKE OR HAVE TIME FOR.

If You Own a Tape Recorder . . .

Make a tape of your voice giving yourself the instruction for each of the 10 steps. Be sure to include the reminder of how many times to repeat each step.

And, above all, include the reminder to rest for 20 seconds with your eyes closed. THEN LEAVE 20 SECONDS OF TAPE BLANK BEFORE GOING ON TO THE NEXT STEP!

You now have at your disposal, to use whenever you like, a *self-instruction relaxation tape.* It offers you a more direct way of learning and practicing the technique than simply memorizing the steps.

Interestingly enough, some people like to have a spouse or lover or friend make the recording rather than making it themselves. Perhaps the voice of a trusted—or intimidating?—other person issues a more effective command instruction to some people. It's a matter of personal preference.

Relaxation can be a powerful tool not only as a calming influence before encountering a dreaded situation, but also after such an encounter. Relaxation *after* the fact can help still the phobic effects of a traumatic event. It can act as a preventive against the development of a phobia as well as its possible expansion into all-encompassing agoraphobia.

In contemporary society where new-found fears breed everywhere, relaxation is of immense value in helping to counter such fears as cancerphobia, homophobia and nucleophobia.

Above all, though, it can be a lifesaver to a mugging or burglary victim who may suffer not only the loss of personal possessions, but also physical harm, and potentially long-lasting psychological scars that barely conceal a phobic fear of crime . . .

Criminophobia

The perception here is that criminals lurk everywhere so that you dread going anywhere lest you become the target.

While it is true that crime is abundant, it is not abundant everywhere. And even where it is more likely to be abundant, the phobic's perception of peril is many times greater than the actual danger.

New York Mayor Ed Koch pointed out why when he spoke of the psychological impact of crime in the subway, much intensified because of the confined space:

"You don't feel that you can run and you feel alone and extremely vulnerable," he said. "You feel a greater fear in your mind, your heart, your stomach, and in your gut.

"It may be just as bad in the street, but at least it's a wide open space."

The reality then is that New York City's subways may very well be less than reliable in terms of safety, but you can't let that take control of your life. You have to keep a tight rein on your perceptions in order to remain cautious, but not phobic.

Unless you do, you can become paralyzed by fear, either because you've become sensitized by news of crime or were victimized yourself.

When Dr. Gilbert Geis, a sociologist and crime expert, interviewed more than a hundred victims of crime at California State College, he concluded, "Their lives often change because they become traumatized by fear. They draw the world around themselves like a circle, deliberately limiting their freedom.

"They think twice before getting into an elevator, or maybe walk up many flights of stairs instead of using elevators at all. They put three or four locks on their doors. Some buy guns.

"They begin to see the world differently, far more apprehensively after the scare of being robbed or burglarized, or after hearing about someone who was."

Some react more intensely than others. A nervous person may become overwhelmed by fear that reaches phobic proportions. But even the coolest, most sophisticated individual is bound to be shaken severely when caught by surprise and subjected to violence or merely threatened with violence.

Dr. Lee R. Steiner is a New York City psychologist of national prominence who devised an unusual psychic relaxation technique to cope with the aftereffects of herself becoming a mugging victim.

"I'm the kind of person who was reared never to be afraid," she says. "I never was anxious in my home, nor in the streets. Many times I would appear on late-night radio or television broadcasts and come home alone at two in the morning without a worry in my head."

What happened that changed that perception?

"One evening I attended a concert at Carnegie Hall not far from my home. Returning home, I was in a gorgeous mood," she recalls, "humming this beautiful melody to myself. I stopped off at an all-night delicatessen to buy something. It was a block and a half away from where I lived.

"I was still humming when I turned the corner of my street, which was quite dark. I had a bag of food on one arm, my purse on the other, and nothing but music on my mind. Then suddenly, out of nowhere . . . something hit me on the head.

"I saw sparks and felt myself falling down hard onto the sidewalk. My arm felt like it was being pulled out of its socket, and in the split second before I passed out I saw a shape tearing at my handbag."

Her head hurt for some time. She learned later that she had been hit with a rubber hose or a stocking stuffed with sand—leaving no clear marks or cracks on her skull. But she suffered a contusion under her skull. In time, it healed.

What didn't heal so quickly were the emotional effects. Amazingly, however, she had no immediate emotional reaction.

"It was the first time in my life that any violence had been directed at me and I didn't know what to make of it," she explains. "The whole thing was beyond my comprehension until one night I woke up in a cold sweat, panicky, and that began to happen night after night for weeks."

Being a psychologist, she was in a better position than the average person to find some means to overcome her terrifying symptoms, but says, "I think the kind of person who's very anxious by nature, middle-class, unaccustomed to violence, could go crazy after such a traumatic experience."

Here is an adaptation of the psychic relaxation technique Dr. Steiner devised to help transform phobic fear into peace-of-mind after a traumatic experience. It is available in full on a Folkways Record and Cassette entitled "Enhancing Psychic Energy."

One of the key elements of this technique is a relaxation exercise we will call . . .

Countdown to Reality

Dr. Steiner explains it as a method of emotional healing that restores the nervous system and the brain to a state of optimum efficiency and tranquility.

Pick a quiet spot. Indoors or outdoors makes no difference so long as it's a quiet spot. Sit comfortably in a favorite chair, or if you're outdoors, you may prefer to sit on the grass and lean back against a rock or whatever. But you must feel comfortable.

Stretch out your legs and rest them on your heels so that you can wave your feet back and forth, and wiggle your toes.

Now look at an object straight ahead of you that you can focus on. It can be anything that you can keep your eyes on comfortably, not a moving object.

Stare at it while you do deep-breathing exercises such as the ones described previously. If you stare at something long enough while breathing regularly and deeply, you will commence to relax to the point where you will want to close your eyes.

Now, with your eyes closed and your entrance into a relaxed state, breathe normally. Let your imagination take over. Visualize the most peaceful place that you can imagine. It can by any place on earth or in heaven. Concentrate on that image, more and more intensely, until you begin to feel completely enveloped by that very peaceful environment.

And now comes the countdown that will help bring you deeper and deeper into a state of relaxation. When you reach the ultimate in relaxation, you will actually feel a warm flow of psychic energy soothing your mind and body.

You are now to count backwards very slowly from fifteen to zero because you're going down, not up—down into deeper and deeper relaxation.

With that lovely visual image clear in your mind and your body at ease, intensify your concentration by counting—silently, slowly—and thinking of nothing else. Just that lovely picture in your mind as you count off . . . 15 . . . 14 . . . 13 . . . and so on until you reach zero.

Once you have mastered this method, you should find yourself mentally and physically relaxed and free of irrational or inappropriately magnified fears.

This requires regular practice. Dr. Steiner recommends a half-hour each day for two weeks to enhance your own psychic energy and make this self-healing relaxation technique dissipate the phobic effects of a traumatic experience.

Now let's look at the reverse side of the coin—the value of utilizing relaxation as a calming influence *before* facing what your mind tells you will be a terrifying experience, so terrifying that you prefer to avoid facing it.

But there are times when that may not be possible or desirable. For example . . .

When You Have to Fly

Letters published in the travel sections of newspapers and magazines often ask for help in finding substitute means of getting to places that are reachable only by airplane.

Unfortunately for aerophobes, acceptable substitutes may not be available, or may require enormous difficulty or expense.

In one such letter, a desperate aerophobe wrote that fear of flying kept her from seeing her sick parents in Puerto Rico and she wanted to know if there was another way to get there from New Jersey.

The only other way, of course, would be by sea, but there is no regular passenger service available. She would either have to charter a ship, at outrageous expense, or try to work out a deal with a cruise ship that made stops at Puerto Rico to let her off and then return on another ship heading back.

It would take a lot of effort to work out such a tricky deal, the cost would be high, and scheduling problems could make for a lot of uncertainty.

Still, to the confirmed aerophobe, all those difficulties might be preferable to flying.

It shouldn't be. It needn't be. A well-planned relaxation exercise—before booking the flight—could reduce anticipatory fear down to a level that would make flying the preferred choice.

This can be done despite the horror stories one hears about, reads about and witnesses on television. Yes, there are crashes, near-misses, skyjackings and bomb scares. This makes news. What doesn't make news are the thousands of flights that take place daily without incident.

Airport security has been tightened and airplane officials have become very sensitized to the merest suggestion that something may be amiss.

To cite just one example, a jet that had just taken off was immediately ordered back when the airline learned that a passenger had hurriedly jumped off the plane before take-off, leaving his luggage behind.

The passengers were quickly led off the plane, and a bomb squad searched the plane and the luggage aboard. It was then discovered that the passenger who had left had done so only because he'd become terribly ill. He hadn't planted a bomb. He just couldn't cope with the prospect of flying. At the last minute, his extreme aerophobia had caused him to panic!

If this unfortunate fellow had employed relaxation as a calming preventive, he would very likely not have had such an extreme panic reaction. And he would certainly have spared his fellow passengers—and the flight crew—a lot of anxiety, a perfectly natural response to an incident of this kind even among non-phobics.

"Life always has risks of some kind," says Captain Tom Bunn, a United Airlines pilot who has developed home-study cassette tapes for people with aerophobia who cannot attend his SOAR seminars in person. "There is a risk in everything we do, every day. Nothing is absolutely certain and it's self-deception to believe otherwise."

He doesn't deny that there is some risk in flying, but he emphasizes that statistics bear out the contention that "no other means of travel—not cars, not trains, not even walking—even approaches the modern jetliner in safety."

Why then are there so many aerophobes?

"These are people who make unrealistic demands on themselves," he says. "They are very concerned about their self-image. And in order to have a good self-image, they convince themselves that they should be able to do anything without feeling anything.

"What they feel is fear. It's perfectly natural, perfectly normal. They're also more intelligent than most people and more imaginative.

"Well, it doesn't seem intelligent to them to put themselves into a situation where they can't feel absolutely sure they're safe, and their imagination makes them think the worst calamity will befall them. So they try to control the uncontrollable, a fear so magnified that it becomes overwhelming.

"Their unrealistic mental perception puts their body in a state of alertness and evokes physical symptoms all phobic persons are familiar with—rapid breathing, a racing heart, clammy sweat, white knuckles, and jellied legs."

To eliminate these distressful phobic responses, they have to realize that however great their fear may be, it is not infinite.

"If you could take that fear out of your head, put it on the table and measure it with a ruler," says Captain Bunn, "you'd see how small it really is and how big you really are. You just imagine your fear to be enormous. In point of fact, it is very limited in size and can only grow to that limit and no further.

"Instead of spending all your energy trying to control it and suffering physical symptoms as a consequence, let go of it. Only when you let go are you really in control of your life. Let the pilot worry about the plane. He's qualified, you aren't. And he's just as interested in his well-being as you are in yours."

The way to let go is by preparing yourself before booking your flight through . . .

A Two-Stage Relaxation Technique

Stage One is a simple breathing exercise. It is the start of relaxation.

Seat yourself comfortably without crossing your legs or your arms. You may want to cross them to feel more at ease. Don't do it, because this is a defensive tactic. Let your defenses down and give up that bit of control. Keep your feet on the floor and let your arms hang loose.

Now breathe in and hold it while you count "One thousand and one, one thousand and two, one thousand and three"—which adds up to about 3 seconds. Then exhale gently.

Pause briefly. Then repeat the breathing exercise half a dozen times.

Stage Two is a simple motion exercise. Stretch out your arms and let your wrists hang free.

Now shake them, your arms and your wrists, as if they were the wings of a bird. Do this a dozen times. Then let them rest.

Now rotate your shoulders, first forward in a rotary motion, then back in a rotary motion. This will release the tension from your neck muscles. Do this half a dozen times forward, then half a dozen times backward.

You should now feel relaxed and in control of yourself without really trying consciously for control. It could help you, if you practice, to bring your fear down to where you will be able to manage making a flight.

And here is a plus—you can do this exercise on the plane *during the flight* to shake off residual tensions aroused by the sounds of the airplane, from the announcements by the pilot and the attendants to the whir of the engines when revved and the thump of the landing gear when raised after takeoff and lowered before landing.

Keep in mind the importance of relaxation exercises as a calming influence before, after or during a fear-provoking situation.

Remember that the key to relaxation is practice. Choose the technique that you find most compatible with your personality and keep at it. And if you find anxiety and tension building up when you're at home because you have to do something that frightens you, make use of strategically-placed reminders that we'll call...

Red Flag Alerts

Get a bunch of little gummed stickers and print on them in bold red ink: "Do a Relaxation Exercise!"

Place these stickers in strategic spots where you are likely to encounter symptoms arising from having to do what scares you.

If you get jumpy answering the telephone or when having to make a call, plant a Red Flag Alert sticker on every phone in your home. If you become fearful when the doorbell rings or when you have to go out, stick a Red Flat Alert on the door and on the wall along the route you take to reach the door. If you tremble when you have to walk the dog, put a Red Flag Alert on his collar.

Look around you to find spots where you feel vulnerable, perhaps being locked in the bathroom or in a walk-in closet. Stick a Red Flag Alert memo there.

This may not cure your phobia but it will help to relieve its terrifying effects. At least until you find a permanent cure.

You'll find it, starting on the next page. . . .

Chapter 7

How to Seize Control for Good

SOME PHOBIAS do not yield to Quick-Fix solutions or relaxation exercises alone. Such remedies can offer only temporary relief for extensive phobic apprehensiveness that has become an integral part of one's life.

If you are in this category, no matter what your phobia might be, consider the previous chapters a prelude to cure. Now we are going to deal with treatment techniques—proven and tested by foremost phobia specialists—that may be the "something more" you need to erase your phobia for good.

This chapter picks up where the others left off. It will give you a choice of treatment modalities because there are more ways than one to cure a phobia.

Which is right for you?

That depends on your phobia, how crippling it is, and the nature of your personality. You'll be given tips to help you decide. Of particular help will be questions that you can ask yourself. For example . . .

Do you consider yourself a very independent person? Are you a pill-popper, rushing to the aspirin bottle at the first sign of a cold or headache? Do you feel more comfortable taking directions than giving them? Do you have a sense of humor? Are you a trend-setter? A high-tech aficionado? A health-and-fitness advocate? How suggestible are you?

Your answers to these and other questions can help you pinpoint the particular technique most appropriate and most effective for you.

Or you may find that several techniques, used in conjunction with one another, would be more applicable and more effective.

It is because you are unique, no matter what you may have in common with other phobic persons, that you must be offered such a choice. All phobia therapy will help, but some will be more helpful than others.

Dr. Arnold Binder, an innovator of programs in Social Ecology and Psychology at the University of California in Irvine, has pointed out that people are likely to choose a therapy technique that meshes with their life-style because "for it to work, it must carry faith, hope and the expectation of success."

So you can't go wrong, however you choose. *You* know what's best for *you!* The exquisite sensitivity that made you phobic in the first place can also serve to rid you of the phobia.

These professional therapeutic techniques have been adapted for do-it-yourself application by those who prefer to do things on their own. Some may prefer professional assistance, however, and some others require it because the technique they elected depends on medical or highly technical intervention for success as well as for safety's sake.

In any case, before you participate in phobia treatment of any kind, you are advised to get a full medical checkup.

"You have to be sure of what you're dealing with," says Dr. Marshall Primack, director of internal medicine at the New York State Psychiatric Institute and in private practice in Manhattan.

He tells, for example, about a middle-aged woman who complained about having panic attacks. But a physical examination revealed that she was suffering from a hyperthyroid condition. When that was treated, her panic attacks all but disappeared.

The medical problem had brought on the anxiety that precipitated panic attacks. After appropriate medical treatment, any residual anxiety or phobia could then be dealt with by any of several phobia treatment techniques.

It takes a perceptive physician to distinguish phobic symptoms from symptoms that mimic those of a true phobic or panic attack. You want to be sure that your dizziness or unsteadiness isn't caused by middle-ear infection, that your hives and shortness of breath aren't the result of sulfite allergy to salad greens or other foods, and that your palpitations and chest pain aren't due to heart disease.

First, rule out the possibility of a medical condition. Then, go all out to rid yourself of the phobia that is really responsible for your terrifying symptoms.

"It's not how long you have had the phobia that counts," according to Dr. Robert DuPont of Georgetown University, "but how badly you want to overcome it and how much effort you put into doing so."

One of the best ways to overcome it is to confront it little by little in a very special way, and this very special way we call . . .

The "Stepladder" Cure

Here is a technique you can do by yourself if you have a good sense of imagination and have mastered any one of the relaxation exercises described in the previous chapter.

The formal name of this remedy is systematic hierarchical desensitization. In simple English, this means facing up to what you fear step-by-step—from what is least threatening to what is most threatening. As you go from the bottom of the "stepladder" to the top, you pause to relax between steps.

You never actually confront whatever it is that you're afraid of. You do it all in your mind by visual imagery. You imagine the thing you fear—rung by rung—as you ascend the "stepladder" that you have built for yourself.

Say, for example, that you're afraid of bridges. Ask yourself what you find least frightening about bridges, and what you find most frightening. In between the least and the most frightening possibilities, make a list of increasingly threatening situations that lead from one to the other. At the very top of your "stepladder" should be what you consider to be the most awful thing that could happen.

You can put as many rungs in that ladder as you need to be able to reach the top without experiencing any anxiety. Just remember to relax completely between rungs. Step-by-step is the way to go.

But if you should panic when you attempt to reach the next step, you must *go back* to the first step and *start all over again!*

Now here is a typical "stepladder" cure for bridge phobia. You must begin by seating yourself in a comfortable chair, dimming the lights, and freeing your mind from all distractions. Then you must do an initial relaxation exercise to free your muscles of tension. Now you are ready to desensitize yourself to bridge phobia just by imagining the increasingly threatening steps of your "stepladder":

1) Imagine yourself driving *past* a bridge.
   RELAX!
2) Imagine yourself driving *toward* a bridge.
   RELAX!
3) Imagine yourself driving *across* a bridge.
   RELAX!
4) Imagine that the bridge is *swaying* in the wind.
   RELAX!
5) Imagine your car being *stalled* on the bridge.
   RELAX!
6) Imagine yourself *stranded*—the only car on the bridge.

If you feel calm after taking the last step, you should be able to drive across a bridge without fear. But take your first drive with a trusted friend or relative.

This technique of alternate relaxation and visualization in a systematic approach can overcome other phobias as well, but you must first isolate the thing you fear most and work on that.

In other words, you may suffer from multiple phobias—and most phobics do—but if you get rid of just one, the one that troubles you most—the others might vanish with it or at least become easier to unload using the same technique.

However, you may not be the sort of person whose imagination is vivid enough to make the basic "stepladder" cure work for you. If that is the case, you may require help from someone who can lead you—little by little—into the actual phobic situation. And this we call . . .

The "Partnering" Cure

It is based on a method devised by Dr. Manuel Zane, a psychiatrist, at his Phobia Clinic at the White Plains Medical Center in New York.

A professional therapist, a recovered phobic, or even a concerned friend or relative can be your partner to lend you support. Imagining a phobic situation is one thing, but actually entering into it is another. You can't do it alone.

Nevertheless, you still use the "stepladder" build-up for gradual indoctrination into the heart of your phobic fear. You begin by touching base with things that don't excite too much apprehensiveness and work your way gradually to where you feel comfortable with whatever scares you most.

And instead of using relaxation exercises as you go from step to step, you use Quick-Fix strategies to help you manage the irrational thoughts that impede your advance to the next step. Any of the Quick-Fix strategies described in an earlier chapter can get you over the hump, as it were, and provide sufficient comfort to enable you to advance—with a partner—to the next step of the hierarchy you have laid out for yourself.

Here is an example of how this version of "partnering" might work for a claustrophobic who panics in elevators. To begin, you must first choose a suitable person to accompany you, and then follow this step-by-step hierarchy:

1) Enter the lobby of a building, apartment house or office building, where there is an elevator.
2) Slowly approach the elevator.
3) Push the "Up" button, but when it arrives at your floor, at the lobby, don't get on, just wait and watch the doors open.

4) Again, push the "Up" button, but this time get on the elevator and ride up to the first floor, then walk back down.
5) Again, in the lobby, push the "Up" button, and take the elevator to the top floor, and down again to the lobby.

That completes the cycle. You've reached the top rung of your "stepladder"—not in your imagination, but in reality—with the support of a trusted someone, *and* with help from various Quick-Fix strategies that enabled you to advance to the next step. Now you should be able to go it alone.

In selecting someone to accompany you, it's important that you pick a person who will reassure you as you move from step to step, and compliment you on your progress.

There is yet another way of using the "stepladder" cure, without a partner, but not quite by yourself. You do have a companion—but your companion is a machine, a tape-recorder. So this we call . . .

The "Me-to-Me" Cure

With the help of a tape recorder, you construct a "stepladder" that takes you from the least to the most terrifying aspect of your phobia—with 20 seconds of tape left blank between steps!

In those 20 seconds, you need not relax, nor need you resort to a Quick-Fix stratagem. You need only pause and contemplate how you are going to reply to the *incomplete statement* you recorded.

Let us suppose that you have a fear of flying. Now write down, in some detail, what it is that bothers you about taking a jet. Put your thoughts in order so that they go from what you find least to most threatening, as in the previous "stepladder" configurations. For example:

"When I think of flying, I start to sweat. The trip to the airport makes my heart race faster. One look at the plane makes me panic. Inside the plane, I feel trapped when I fasten my seat belt. When the motors start, my head throbs. On leaving the ground, I can't catch my breath. If the ride gets bumpy, I feel like passing out. When the plane comes in for a landing, I feel sure I'm going to die. Only when the plane lands and stops do I finally feel calm."

That is a detailed narrative of aerophobia. What you must do with it is transfer it to tape. Read what you have written into the microphone—but *every time you're about to mention your fear reaction, stop talking for 20 seconds.* Then, continue with your narrative.

During those 20 seconds of blank tape, when you play it back to yourself, you will be able to contemplate the anxiety you experience at various stages of your projected flight. As you replay this tape, you will find yourself able to extinguish fear on a step-by-step basis. You will become habituated, in small doses, to situations that inspire fear in you and, as one after another arouses less anxiety, ultimately free yourself of even the worst fear that you can think of.

This is how to put together the tape of the narrative just described: "When I think of (20 SECONDS OF DEAD TAPE) flying, I start to (20 SECONDS OF DEAD TAPE) sweat. The trip to the airport makes my heart (20 SECONDS OF DEAD TAPE) race faster. One look at the plane makes me (20 SECONDS OF DEAD TAPE) panic . . ." And so on.

No matter which of these "stepladder" cures you decide to use (perhaps all of them?), if you can make it to the top rung even when something goes wrong and leaves you feeling *vulnerable but not panic-stricken,* you can congratulate yourself on having overcome your phobia!

Do machines fascinate you? Do you prefer to take your exercise on a piece of machinery that does your bending and stretching for you? Are you gung-ho about computers and other high-tech gadgetry?

If you answered yes to most of these questions, then you may be a good candidate for . . .

The "High-Tech" Cure

Its formal name is biofeedback. It helps you gain control over phobic symptoms that affect your mind and body by letting you know what is going on under your skin and inside your head.

It does this by hooking you up—painlessly and non-invasively—to a bunch of electronic instruments with a biofeedback specialist by your side to act as your guide. The Biofeedback Certification Institute of America (BCIA) is the professional organization to which all qualified practitioners belong.

To understand how it works, forget about the gadgetry for a moment and listen to how therapist Howard Kay explains it.

"If you looked in a mirror," he says, "that would be biofeedback. The mirror is reflecting back to you information you can understand and use immediately.

"One look tells you if your make-up is on correctly, your hair properly set, your dress appropriate. If not, you can make changes based upon your reflection. In the same way, you can change your behavior by the feedback you get, not from a mirror, but from electronic instruments."

Tiny sensors are taped to your skin, on your brow, on your hands, and attached to instruments that measure minuscule changes in muscle tension, brain wave patterns, skin temperature and sweat gland activity. You feel nothing. There is no danger of electrical shock. When the session is over, the sensors are simply lifted off.

But while you are connected, you will be seated comfortably in an easy chair listening to sounds that change in tone or pitch, and watching lights that change color—all of these changes being reflections of the biological signals coming from your body and mind.

You do nothing except listen to the sounds and watch the lights. If the sounds are too loud, you may prefer that they be softer or even totally silent. If the lights are bright red and flickering, you may prefer them to remain still and perhaps change to a more soothing color.

All you have to do to make these things happen is to want them to happen. You do this by what Howard Kay calls "passive attention."

"You don't actively strive to make these changes," he says. "You attend to the process, not to the outcome."

Dr. Elliott Wineburg is a psychiatrist and hypnotist, and the director of the Associated Biofeedback Medical Group in New York City. He likens biofeedback training to learning to ride a bicycle.

"When you first get up on your bicycle, you may have trouble staying up," he says. "So you try again, and this time you stay up. In fact, every time you ride your bicycle, you stay upright. You don't know why you are able to do it, but you are.

"Biofeedback works the same way. Here we use state-of-the-art instrumentation that monitors your biological signals and converts them to a computerized video display that gives you feedback on a TV screen."

You watch a line that goes up and down. At the same time, the sound you hear through a set of headphones also get louder and softer. And the lower the line, the softer the sound, the more complimentary will be your therapist: "Look where you are now, that's very, very good!"

Yes, you're right if you've guessed that reward and punishment, sometimes called operant conditioning, plays a part in making biofeedback work. So you will need a guide in addition to the gadgetry, someone to tell you how you're doing to keep your attention focused on the feedback display of your progress.

The remarkable thing about biofeedback therapy is the way it works without your doing anything, or seemingly without your doing anything. It doesn't work on everyone. But when it does, you know it, even though you don't know why. But, just like that, no more feelings of terror.

According to biofeedback specialists, you can literally let fear slip through your fingers. You do it simply by warming your fingers.

"It isn't possible to warm your fingers and get into a panic reaction," says Dr. Wineburg.

"If I can teach patients to warm their fingers, they will create the opposite of an emergency response. And once they've learned how to do it, they can do it at any time to interdict the biological mechanism that used to lead to a panic reaction."

You can try it for yourself. Here is all you need to know

about . . .

The "Fingertip" Cure

The idea of warming one's fingertips is based on the fact that such warming increases one's peripheral circulation. It is something the Yogis of India know very well. They can alter their skin temperature to such a fine point that they can actually make one finger hot and another cold, so complete is their control over their bodies.

That control extends to their remarkable ability to induce deep muscle relaxation everywhere in their body and in their nervous system. Somehow, they become able to alter the messages that go from their brain to all parts of their body and achieve absolute serenity which, of course, is the opposite of phobic fear and panic.

In the matter of finger-warming, biofeedback specialist Howard Kay explains: "The normal peripheral skin temperature ranges from about 87 to 89 degrees. When the temperature goes down, the blood vessels become constricted and the level of anxiety goes up."

So, to bring down the anxiety level, you must raise your skin temperature. And if you can do it with your fingers, you have probably the simplest, most inexpensive biofeedback technique available at your fingertips!

Buy yourself an ordinary outdoor thermometer with a cardboard backing that displays readings above 100 degrees. It must have a bulb at its base that you can grasp easily between your thumb and forefinger.

Shake the thermometer to get the mercury down, the lower the better, so that you can make it climb up dramatically. At least be sure it registers well below the 80-degree mark.

Now grasp the bulb between your thumb and forefinger. You want the temperature to rise above 90 degrees, as far above as possible.

Now all you can do to make that happen is to want it to happen, that's all. So just squeeze the bulb and keep your eye on the column of mercury, watching it rise. That's biofeedback, right there.

Keep practicing this technique whenever you feel the urge or whenever you begin to experience anxious feelings that you can't account for, or feelings of terror that are out of proportion to your actual situation.

According to biofeedback theory, the more you raise your fingertip temperature above 90 degrees, the more you will find yourself in control of your feelings and consequent physical symptoms.

When you become able to do so on a regular basis, you will be able to ditch the thermometer and warm your fingertips at will without requiring feedback from the thermometer itself.

Now here is a method for conquering phobias that could be very effective for people who are highly suggestible. And this method is called . . .

The "Superconsciousness" Cure

"Hypnotism," according to Dr. Elliot Wineburg, "puts you in a state of superconsciousness. It is like putting your mind under a magnifying glass to intensify its focus.

"It's very helpful for those who don't do well on biofeedback alone, but it is also effective on its own for some phobics."

Much depends on how suggestible you are because that will help determine how hypnotizable you are. Here is a little test that can help you find out for yourself. But you will need help from someone whose authority you respect.

Have that someone order you to clasp your hands tightly. Then do so.

Now have that someone make very clear to you that when he or she finishes counting slowly from 1 to 10, your hands will stick together like glue!

If you are suggestible, by the time that other person completes the count to 10, you will find it difficult, perhaps almost impossible, to separate your hands. Should that happen, you can consider yourself very suited to becoming hypnotized out of your phobic fear.

Whoever you choose as your hypnotherapist follows essentially these three steps: 1) He gradually induces a trance state. 2) He makes suggestions while you're in that state to relax you and alter your phobic perceptions. 3) He makes post-hypnotic suggestions to extend their good effects after he takes you out of the trance.

Dr. Wineburg, serving as president of the New York Society for Clinical Hypnosis, said that a post-hypnotic suggestion could be as simple as saying, "Whenever you feel the presence of fear, just brush it away by brushing your hand over your forehead as I'm doing now to put yourself at ease."

There is nothing really mysterious about the mumbo jumbo that makes hypnotism work. It is simply the highly repetitive nature of the monotonous monologue that does it: "You're getting tired tired, sleepy sleepy . . ." If you're suggestible, you're bound to become tired and sleepy!

It is the post-hypnotic suggestions that continue to reinforce the treatment process and smooth away your phobic fears. The magic of the words spoken by the hypnotist play upon your suggestibility and becomes a positive influence that counters the symptoms of phobic fear.

Your hypnotherapist may record a special tape for you to take home with you that will enable you to hypnotize yourself and—this is most important—have a built-in alarm system that will enable you to snap out of a self-imposed hypnotic trance state. It could be no more than a post-hypnotic suggestion that not only takes you out of the trance but also enables you to deal realistically with your most distressing phobic symptom.

But the magic of words alone may not be enough for some phobia victims. They may prefer the "magic" of a pill, especially if they suffer from panic attacks and the crippling effects of agoraphobia.

Well, modern medicine has now made possible . . .

The "Push-Button Drug" Cure

Few life incidents are more terrifying than a sudden panic attack for which there seems to be no apparent cause. The skin tingles, it feels hot and cold by turns, the head swims with vertigo, and the heart thumps loudly in one's chest.

In fact, the cardiovascular effects have been a special interest of Dr. Drew Gaffney who is not only a cardiologist investigating anxiety disorders at the University of Texas Health Science Center in Dallas, but was also appointed to the crew of America's space shuttle to conduct research for NASA.

"When people become frightened, they have cardiac symptoms," says Dr. Gaffney, "because the heart may beat too fast for the body's 'computer' to regulate."

Palpitations could result from a cardiac abnormality, other medical conditions or from nothing more than a panic disorder. A clear distinction must be made.

Women in particular have a common condition known as mitral valve prolapse. This generally benign disorder of the heart valve may mimic panic disorder because about half of those who have it complain of having palpitations. But these are two different conditions and it is unclear which, if any, triggers the other. What they have in common are the palpitations, and these are treatable in both conditions.

Dr. Jack Gorman and his colleagues at the New York State Psychiatric Institute, the oldest medical research institute in the United States, says, "It is now possible to eliminate panic attacks and alleviate phobic avoidance in almost all patients with panic disorder, so the disorder is among the most treatable of all psychiatric illnesses."

How is it done?

With an anti-panic pill!

It has been found that a drug called *imipramine* ("Tofranil"), one of a family of drugs known as tricyclic anti-depressants, can block the panic attack. A similar drug is *desipramine* ("Norpramin").

No, they don't work with the first dose you take. But if you take such a drug as prescribed by your doctor for a brief period of time, they will then have the "push-button" effect built into the medication.

"Successful pharmacologic blockade of panic attacks is the only treatment that many patients with panic disorder and agoraphobia need," say the researchers at the New York State Psychiatric Institute.

And for people who don't respond to the above drugs, there is another class of drugs called Mono-Amine Oxidase Inhibitors (MAOI) that can do the job. One of these is *phenelzine* ("Nardil") but there are others in the same drug family.

In addition, researchers in anxiety disorders at NYSPI and in the psychiatry departments of Yale University and the Connecticut Mental Health Center have found still another drug, *alprazolam* ("Xanax"), that is effective in warding off a panic attack.

What all these drugs have in common is their ability to shut off the overly-sensitive alarm system of a panic disorder sufferer that goes off when there is no life-threatening situation present to trigger it. When you shut off that alarm system, you shut off the panic attack.

But that may not bring your worry to a full stop. You could be like the heart attack victim who, although declared fit and ready to return to work, won't get out of bed because he worries that another heart attack is imminent.

So, even though you're assured that you won't get another panic reaction, you may still be *fearful* that you will. This is called anticipatory anxiety, in which case an anti-panic drug alone may not be enough. You may have to go on to the "Stepladder" Cure or the "Partnering" Cure or some other treatment strategy in keeping with your personality to overcome any anticipatory anxiety and lick your phobia once and for all.

This is very important for you to keep in mind if panic attacks have increased your avoidance behavior to a point where you have become agoraphobic. First, eliminate the panic attacks with an appropriate anti-panic drug, and then go on to one of the other treatment techniques to desensitize yourself to be rid forever of all groundless fear and anxiety.

For what are called Simple Phobias—fear of one particular thing such as height, closed spaces or animals—there are available many "push-button" drugs called minor tranquilizers. Among others, these include drugs from the *benzodiazepam* drug family such as "Valium", "Serax" and "Librium."

They don't cure, but they can decrease anxiety symptoms substantially. Perhaps their greatest value lies in the value that a phobic sufferer places on them. You can keep them around without ever taking them just to feel secure in having them around.

Phobics who respond to the "magic" of a pill may get all the help they need from something new, "Endorphs"® that contain *no drugs* but may act in ways that mimic the brain's own natural anti-stressors, the endorphins.

The social phobic who suffers from having to appear in public—eating, cashing a check, performing—can be helped by a quite different "push-button" drug called a "beta-blocker." It is basically a drug intended to treat hypertension and angina but has been found to be helpful in treating social phobia symptoms.

These include shakiness, sweating, blushing, and so on. The heart pounds fast and furiously when the social phobic is placed in a vulnerable situation, whether it be a business meeting or on the concert stage.

Well, this is a pill that can stop the pounding heart and reduce the other symptoms along with it. Chemically, this drug is known as *propranalol* ("Inderal"), and a newer but similar drug called *atenolol* ("Tenormin"), both of which have been found to serve the same purpose which is, essentially, to reduce stage fright and the fear of embarrassing oneself in public. Check with your doctor!

So, for the phobic who prefers the "magic" of a pill to any other kind of treatment, there is much to choose from. On the other hand, there are phobics—and you may be one—whose treatment choice is based on a burning desire to know more about himself or herself.

Does this sound like you?

If it does, you may find just what you're looking for in . . .

The "Talking" Cure

Yes, you guessed correctly. This is the treatment technique known more familiarly as "psychotherapy," or more classically as "psychoanalysis."

Some think this approach is passé.

Wrong! It is only passé for those who do not share the believers' faith in such treatment or who have no desire to probe deeply into the sources of their phobic symptoms. All well and good for them. But maybe not for you.

Are you the kind of person who wants to know the "why" of everything—why you have mixed feelings about your spouse, your parents, your children? And perhaps why you feel upset when there is no reason you can think of as to why you should feel upset? Or why you have to spend more money than you can afford in order to feel good, or to stint when you don't have to in order to feel good?

In short, if you suffer from inner conflicts that arouse anxiety, and that may be responsible for the irrational fears that make you phobic, you may prefer to purge yourself of these conflicts rather than simply deal with their effects.

If that is the case, psychotherapy may be just what the doctor ordered to cure you of your phobia. You could visit a medically trained psychoanalyst once a week or, preferably and if you can afford it, three or five times a week, on a one-to-one basis. Or you could choose treatment by a psychotherapist with no medical training but who possesses a Ph.D. in psychology, or no more than a Master's Degree in social work, or no degree at all—yet is nevertheless permitted to practice just about everywhere in the U.S.A.

Aside from academic distinctions, if you and your therapist mesh well together, you are sure to get a closer look at the emotional meaning of your phobic symptoms. It comes about through what is known as "insight-oriented" therapy.

All this means is that when you find someone whom you trust, and whose expertise you respect, and pour out to that person your innermost feelings—things you haven't dared to admit to yourself, let alone to others—you will already have taken some of the steam out of your pent-up feelings.

When, in return, your therapist hands you back an interpretation of those feelings so that you finally begin to recognize their emotional effects upon your psyche, you will feel a great sense of relief. In psychoanalytic terms, this is called "catharsis."

It is simply an unloading of hurtful emotional baggage that, until it was explained to you in terms you could comprehend and absorb, became converted into irrational fears that made you phobic.

For some, the "Talking" cure may be all the treatment they need. Just being able to talk about the painful or unacceptable thoughts, impulses and desires with a concerned but objective person can reduce their emotional effects. And the insight into these feelings that the objective, emotionally uninvolved therapist passes along can restore sufficient emotional balance and control to cure the phobia.

If your problem is social phobia, it's very likely that whenever you go anywhere, you try to re-arrange your body to put yourself at ease. You probably throw out your chest, draw your head back and square your shoulders, but all that does is make you feel weak in the knees and intensify your anxiety. It's a mistake to "straighten up."

A better way to use your body and overcome your phobia is a technique we call . . .

The "Heads Up" Cure

It is based on a remarkable discovery by an actor named F.M. Alexander who suffered from stage fright and hoarseness whenever he had to perform, and so is known professionally as the Alexander Technique.

Professional musicians use it to relieve the occupational hazards of their work, everything from "fiddler's neck" to "harpist's cramp." And it has been acclaimed by such heavyweight thinkers as John Dewey, Aldous Huxley and George Bernard Shaw as a mind-and-body control technique that re-educates the entire nervous system.

In fact, the eminent British philosopher Alfred North Whitehead stressed the importance of viewing one's body as an instrument whose proper functioning can alter one's perception of the world. "Lack of peace in the body," he said, "makes almost impossible the condition known as peace of mind."

There's a strong suggestion there that people with phobia, particularly social phobia, use their bodies incorrectly.

"We react primitively to stress," explains a communications specialist who teaches the Alexander Technique at Carnegie-Mellon University in Pittsburgh. "We pull our heads back, lower our necks into our shoulders and create many breathing and other physical problems for ourselves."

So, with the body not at peace, neither is the mind. That leads to a kind of psycho-social stress that panics social phobics if they have to eat out, sign a check at the bank, make a speech at a business meeting or perform on stage.

No one knows this better than Linda Babits, a pianist, and Hillary Mayers, a singer, co-directors of Alexander Technique Affiliates in New York City who teach this method at their studio and in seminars throughout the world.

"You have to change the way you use your body habitually," says Linda. "The first step is to become aware of what you're doing wrong when you sit or stand. Stop and think about what's happening.

"You'll discover that the way you hold your head and shoulders is putting a lot of strain on your neck and on your spine. That puts your muscles out of synch, and when that happens your mind goes out of synch as well.

"It's not a matter of learning to relax. It's a matter of learning how to balance your head so that it seems to float out of your spine, taking the pressure off the surrounding nerves and restoring muscular harmony."

The best way to understand it is to try it yourself. It's best to have someone help you, but you can also do it alone. Follow these simple steps:

1) Stand upright and spread your legs apart.

2) Say to yourself: "I'm going to allow my spine to organize my body in such a way that everything within me is in harmony."

3) Now that you're aware that you intend to change a habit pattern, stop for a moment and actually say to your brain: "No!"

4) You have instructed your brain to stop ordering your body to follow an old habit pattern because you want to change it.

5) Now, if someone is helping you, have that person spread one hand under your jaw, the other on the back of your neck, to lift your head up and forward, pulling *gently,* and holding it so for several seconds. If you are alone, do it by yourself.

6) Now have your friend let go, or let go yourself.

7) You should experience a lovely feeling of floating, feel taller, and breathe better.

That is the essence of what is called here the "Heads Up" cure. You can feel the difference, but you must keep practicing it until you reach a point where you can do it automatically merely by pausing and saying "No" to your brain. At that point, your brain will tell your body what to do.

"The reason you have to stop and think before you do anything," says Hillary, "is because you have to start with a clean slate to do something new. It's like erasing a neurological blackboard. You do that by stopping, becoming aware, re-training your brain, and then your brain re-trains your body."

Of course you'll do better with help from a certified specialist in the technique who can provide the full gamut of training. But with a bit of persistence, mastering this simple exercise by yourself will enable you to experience the wonderful exhilaration that replaces the fearful anxiety that characterized your social phobia.

But are you more concerned about what goes into your body by way of your mouth than by way of messages from your brain? In short, are you into nutrition?

If you are, then you might find an effective treatment for your phobia in . . .

The "Food for Thought" Cure

An increasing amount of attention is being paid to the effects of the food we eat upon the way we behave. A whole new profession of nutrition therapy has sprung up that emphasizes the role played by various foods, minerals, vitamins and micro-nutrients—not upon our digestive processes, but upon our physical and mental well-being.

The common feeling that these nutrition experts share is that foods influence brain chemistry, and the resultant bio-chemical imbalance—the product of poor nutritional habits—can trigger phobic reactions.

At Cornell University's Nutrition Information Center, for example, Dr. Barbara Levine, the director, stresses the importance of calcium not only for its value in building bones and teeth but also for its role in "nerve impulse conduction, muscle contraction and relaxation."

Dr. Michael Lesser, a physician who practices nutritional medicine in Berkeley, California, goes even farther, reporting "strong similarities between the symptoms of an anxiety attack and the mental symptoms of calcium deficiency."

While this is highly controversial, those who espouse this view recommend taking in more calcium from such foods as milk, dairy products, peas, beans, potatoes, cauliflower, dried figs and molasses.

Some nutritionists regard the mineral magnesium as a calming agent, essential for the nervous system. You can get all you need by making sure to have a good portion of green vegetables in your daily diet.

A new medical specialty, clinical ecology, pioneered by Dr. Theron G. Randolph, a Chicago physician, suggests that "hidden" food allergies could trigger many kinds of disorders, including emotional upsets. The most common offenders are said to be wheat, corn, coffee, yeast, eggs, beef, pork and milk. Traditional allergists, however, maintain that food sensitivities affect few people and their symptoms are limited to itchy skin conditions, abdominal cramps and intestinal upsets.

Caffeine is regarded by some doctors and researchers as a provoker of panic attacks in susceptible persons, possibly by blocking the action of adenosine, a brain chemical that works as a calming agent. Four or five cups of coffee, or the equivalent amount of tea, cola, even chocolate, may trigger panic attacks in some people.

Theories and panaceas of many kinds abound in the burgeoning field of nutrition as practiced by specialists in that area, chiropractors and even some behavioral therapists, psychologists and psychiatrists.

Dr. Julian Herskowitz, of TERRAP, New York, suggests that phobic persons swear off caffeine, alcohol and sugar, and perhaps take a 1,000 milligram capsule of L-Tryptophan daily as a calming agent.

"If you enjoy eating turkey, and feel good after eating a turkey dinner," he says, "it's the L-Tryptophan in the turkey that does it."

A possible link between food and mood was the subject of a recent study at the University of Chicago by a research team headed by Dr. John Crayton, as associate professor of psychiatry.

Volunteers were fed capsules containing powdered wheat, milk and chocolate for a period of eight days. Mood assessments and behavioral and neuropsychological tests were conducted four times each day, while blood chemistry tests and immune system analyses were made twice a day.

Marked changes in mood showed up in two-thirds of the group and there were changes in their immune systems as well. While the results are not definitive, the researchers theorize that substances formed during an immune system reaction might cause local swelling of the brain which could trigger mood swings. In this study, wheat and milk were the culprits.

If you are really into nutrition, and believe that food and mood go hand-in-hand, you'll have no trouble following the foregoing recommendations as a means of helping you overcome the calamitous effects of your phobia.

Then again, you may be the sort who benefits from having been blessed with a fine sense of humor, and it may be more to your liking to try . . .

The "Laugh It Off" Cure

The reason a sense of humor can help you make this remedy work is because if you have that, you will in all likelihood possess a sense of the absurd.

The absurd?

Yes, because this technique deals with fear not by trying to bring it down but by doing just the reverse—making it reach utterly dreadful proportions!

It is a combination of a therapy known as "flooding" and another known as "paradoxical intention," in the adaptation presented here.

To help you better understand the way it can work for you, consider two cases of aerophobia that were dealt with in very different ways . . .

1) Sheila is terrified of flying, and flies only when it is absolutely necessary, and only with her husband along. He tries to calm her terrors by babying her throughout the flight.

She appreciates his concern and pampering but says, "I don't know why but it only makes me worse. The more he babies me, the more frightened I become. He's trying to help me but I feel totally out of control."

2) Brenda is equally terrified of flying. She, too, will fly only when it is absolutely necessary, and only with her husband along. But he doesn't baby her. On the contrary, he tries to scare the life out of her, but in a certain way.

"This plane will never make it," he tells her as he puts an arm around her casually but protectively. "Listen to that engine, I think it just missed a beat! And here we are miles above the ground, all of us here in this little stinking airplane, and we're going to go down, down, down and crash into little bits and pieces all over the place. Smash, crash, bang, boom, whooey for everybody!"

And she begins to laugh—because she finds his thoroughly wild commentary utterly ridiculous. For a while, his remarks increased her tension, her hands shook, her heart pounded, but then her sense of the absurd took over as she realized that her husband's fantasy of disaster was only that—a fantasy.

What her husband did was to exaggerate Brenda's fear to the point of satire.

Clearly, this technique is a no-no for people who tend to become hysterical. For others, it might be eminently appropriate, but it helps to have a caring someone beside you if you want to attempt it by yourself. And you can do that with the help of a tape recorder.

Build up a story about whatever it is that you fear most to a degree where you not only imagine, but actually wish for, the worst possible thing to happen. Write it down and read it back to your tape recorder. Have someone beside you when you record it and when you play it back to yourself.

For example, say that you're afraid of falling . . .

"I'm going up to the top of the Empire State Building. . . . It's crowded and people are pushing against me. . . . I hold onto the railing for protection but it gives way. . . . Oh, I'm falling! . . . Falling floor after floor. . . . I see windows going by. . . . The wind is spinning me around. . . . Now there's the sidewalk coming up at me. . . . I'm going to hit it . . . hard, hard, hard . . . breaking my bones . . . blood splattered everywhere . . . ohhhhhhhhh!"

You're bound to read such a fearsome recitation dramatically and become emotionally drained when you finish. When you play it back—several times, not just once—you'll feel exhausted but relaxed, knowing it was only a fantasy.

Pinch yourself. You'll feel completely whole again, and chances are that you'll forget the pain of the experience that took place only in your mind and be able to laugh away your phobic fear.

Perhaps the one fear above all that cannot be laughed away is erotophobia, the fear of sex, because it not only reaches into the hidden recesses of our private mind but also wages phobic war against our private parts.

If you want pleasure to replace anxiety, and success to replace failure, strike back at your phobia with . . .

The "Super-Touch" Cure

Men and women who avoid sexual intimacy do so for a multitude of reasons. They may think it's dirty, worry that they'll contact venereal disease, or fear that something terrible will happen to their genital organs if they have intercourse.

There are men, for example, who are terrified of inserting themselves into a woman for fear that violent contractions of the vagina will crush the penis. It will no doubt lead to an inability to have an erection. But psychogenic impotence, which is what that is, won't necessarily erase a deep-down desire for sexual pleasure—but without the threat of pain.

Women suffer from similar fears that they will be hurt or damaged if they allow themselves to be penetrated—even though they may have the desire to copulate, and be perfectly okay anatomically. But when penetration is attempted, they close up, substituting fear for fun.

Dr. Helen Singer Kaplan, clinical professor of psychiatry at New York Hospital's Cornell Medical College, is one of the nation's foremost experts in sexual therapy. And she has pointed out that such women are sexually responsive but are "phobic of coitus and vaginal penetration."

She goes on to add, "They may be orgastic on clitoral stimulation, enjoy sexual play, and seek sexual contact as long as this does not lead to intercourse."

And Dr. Julian Herskowitz, the TERRAP therapist, relates the story about a 28-year-old virgin who attributed her fear of penetration to having been told by a gynecologist in her pre-teen years that she had a very small opening in her vagina.

"She really had no fear of sex per se," she says, "but of intimacy, of pain, of being stretched and hurt."

All these cases are best treated by non-verbal forms of communication developed by Masters and Johnson that emphasize the sense of touch.

Gently and gradually, first alone, then together, an exploration of one another's body is made—no words, just touch—more as a means of communication than as a means of sexual pleasuring.

It is a step-by-step touch procedure, including masturbatory techniques that break through personal inhibitions, using whatever fantasy elements may be necessary to evoke sexual stimulation. If Robert Redford turns you on, think of Robert Redford. If your "manhood" is turned on by Tina Turner, let her be the subject of your fantasy.

Neither of them will know what's going on in your head, or anywhere else. Nor will they mind. In fact, if they did know, they might be terribly flattered. So there is no reason to feel shy or ashamed about whatever private thoughts you find enjoyable.

Progress from having a sexual monologue to having a sexual dialogue—still without exchanging a word. All that matters is touch!

The standard procedure is to start out fully clothed and little by little remove articles of clothing from one another, without a word exchanged, and touch here, touch there, in "unimportant" places. Then, taking your time, become more familiar with each other's body, embracing, kissing, exchanging caresses as you commence to explore each other's private parts.

Go slow and easy. Touch is all you want, not satisfaction. Not yet. That is the key to making touch work for you in overcoming a fear of sex. Slow and easy. Time is on your side.

"Take the initiative to do many things that you have felt to be taboo," says Dr. Alexander Runciman, a social psychologist who worked with Masters and Johnson, "and feel the pleasure of being caressed."

The right touch can really be super and put an end to sexual fears and the phobic fantasies that inhibit your experiencing one of the greatest delights of being alive.

Some phobias worsen with age, one's social position, and one's financial situation, and all these are influenced by our contemporary social culture that places great value upon the *appearance* of youth and the vitality associated with it.

This could profoundly affect the way you perceive your body and, hence, the world around you. It was Sigmund Freud himself who first pointed out that the body is the core of a person's psychological identity because "one's *inner* image is formed by one's perception of one's *outer* image."

Well, if this contributes to your phobic apprehensiveness, you probably fear being rejected, even humiliated, socially, careerwise and otherwise.

The most appropriate remedy way be . . .

The "New Image" Cure

It is common knowledge that celebrities turn to plastic surgeons to update their appearance or to correct blemishes that cause them anxiety that interferes with their self-confidence.

Here's a sampling of some who, for one reason or another, opted for a "new image"—Phyllis Diller and Lana Turner (face-lifts), Michael Jackson and Peter O'Toole (noses), Frank Sinatra (hair), Carol Burnett (chin), Mariel Hemingway (breast augmentation) and Eileen Brennan (face repair after an accident).

What is not so well-known is that over 2,000,000 ordinary Americans of both sexes turn to plastic surgeons every year to alter their perceptions by altering their appearance.

According to Dr. Thomas Cash, a psychologist at Old Dominion College in Norfolk, Virginia, women are more susceptible emotionally because appearance counts more in their overall feelings about themselves.

And Daniel Brown, a clinical psychologist at Harvard Medical School, has suggested that poor body image at crucial stages in one's life (adolescence, for example) can lead to a susceptibility to mental disorders later in life.

In other words, poor body image in one's younger years can sow the seeds of phobias in later years. This is why an increasing number of young people are having their noses bobbed before they enter college or the workplace.

One of New York's foremost specialists in cosmetic surgery, Dr. Dennis Barek, conducts a thriving private practice on Manhattan's upper East Side. He recently had to operate on a young business woman who had been brutally mugged while waiting for a bus on Fifth Avenue. Her nose had been bashed in and her face had been slashed with a razor.

"She was in terrible pain physically, and psychologically as well," says Dr. Barek, "because her appearance was of key importance in her career as an executive. And she had had to overcome many obstacles in her climb to the top."

Now, thanks to the miracle of reconstructive surgery and her own indomitable spirit, she is looking good and feeling good again. But perhaps most remarkable is that despite her frightening ordeal, this grateful woman is not phobic about city streets or its bus stops. Her perceptions are realistic, not fraught with fear and apprehensive anxiety.

Few of us are that fortunate. Even minor blemishes, a slight scar, puffy or baggy eyelids, breasts that are too large or too small, a few wrinkles . . . and we feel a sense of shame.

After all, nobody on the TV screen looks this way!

"People have changed and their perceptions have changed," says Dr. Barek. "I used to have patients who were afraid to sit in the waiting room for fear of being seen and recognized. Now they feel good about it."

The shame of having a facelift has given way to the shame of not having one, because the perception is that you have to look the part to feel the part and get the job.

"When they come in for their first consultation," he says, "they invariably say, 'I'm competing with a lot of younger individuals and I don't want to look tired. My neck feels tired, my face feels tired, my eyes feel tired. I want to continue working for many more years and I can't compete if I feel this way.'

"That particular motivation is a very positive one for both men and women over, say, the age of fifty who are fearful of losing career opportunities."

Dr. Barek, who has particular expertise in esthetic surgery, says you can't turn back the clock and lop twenty years off your age, but you can have changes made that will make you look fresher, brighter and more rested. That's what gives you the younger look and the feeling to go with it, the end of fears of being rejected.

How do you know if this treatment technique is right for you?

"Well, let me give you an example of a woman who wanted to have some facial surgery touch-up," he says. "She was very attractive, in her forties, had good skin, and I felt that the amount of change or improvement would be minimal. So it was hard for me to justify the risks and possible complications, and I told her so.

"But she insisted, said that she was being treated by a psychiatrist and that I should talk to him. So I did. He told me this lady was highly perfectionistic, fearful of all kinds of consequences from the slightest imperfection. And it was his professional opinion as a psychiatrist that cosmetic surgery would be beneficial for her.

"So I accepted her as a patient, did the surgery, and she was happy and grateful with the result. The benefit was psychological as well as esthetic."

Another case concerned a teenager so ashamed of her nose that she had withdrawn from all social contact. After surgery, her overjoyed mother said, "She's a different person, really. She has a whole new opinion about herself. She's outgoing, assertive and has lost all her social anxieties."

In choosing this technique for its anti-phobic potential, you must size up carefully the degree to which your appearance affects your self-perception, the degree to which your outer image affects your inner image. And you must have a clear idea of what to expect from cosmetic surgery of any kind.

A facelift, for example, shouldn't be overdone. As Dr. Barek puts it, "Better to have a wrinkle or two than lose your expressiveness."

To help his patients make informed decisions, he is uniquely assisted by a communicator, a registered nurse, who is available to patients to hold their hands and help reinforce warm doctor-patient relations.

"If you want some idea of how you'll look after a facelift," she says, "the surgeon can show you with his hands, pulling on your skin."

And she adds, "Having one can be a kind of self-fulfilling prophecy. If others admire you, you'll feel more self-assured."

Or, as some recovered phobics explain it, the way you look is the way you feel. Or, to put it still another way, the way to a man's heart may be through his stomach, but the way to a phobic's irrational fears may be through that sufferer's perception of his or her body image.

Every cure in this chapter will work for somebody. One or more will surely work for you, to help you seize control for good.

But there is even more good news coming. . . .

Chapter 8

You Are Not Alone

Strange as it may seem, there are advantages to belonging to that very special "club" of some 40 million American men and women who have phobias. The reason is simple.

When only a relatively small number of people suffer from an affliction, that affliction is labeled an "orphan disease" because there is no one to look after it. It doesn't pay the scientific establishment to invest time and money in research because there are too few victims to compensate them for their investment, no matter how successful the outcome might be.

But when some 40 million people are afflicted, you can be sure that a lot of attention will be given that problem!

Phobias are getting more attention every day as specialists in biology and behavior endeavor to find out more and more about them.

So, in addition to the benefits that hopefully you have already realized in this book, you can look forward to further benefits from the . . .

Promising New Research

Enormous attention is being paid to the brain itself in order to learn more about how it works and how to make it work better.

There is good news in a special report from the mental health division of the esteemed National Academy of Sciences which states, "The rapidity with which basic biological principles of brain function are emerging far exceeds even the most optimistic predictions of two decades ago."

At the Veterans Administration Hospital in Honolulu, psychologist Claude Chemtob is looking into the possibility that phobias are more prevalent among left-handed persons and among those with left-handed relatives, since his initial research seems to bear this out.

At the University of California, San Francisco, neuroscientists are trying to discover why some brains can't use their natural braking mechanism—like the brakes in your car—to control their response to perceived danger.

At the Salk Institute's Peptide Biology Laboratory, San Diego, they are searching for a molecule small enough to pass from the bloodstream into the brain to block the sort of stress familiar to every phobic who has ever been trapped in a traffic jam.

And the Upjohn Pharmaceutical Company is testing a new drug for panic attacks and agoraphobia on 1600 people in 15 countries, which has a side benefit of making the world even more aware of phobias and their crippling effects.

A possible connection between "jerky" eye movements and brain disorders is being investigated at the City of Hope's Beckman Research Institute in Los Angeles and elsewhere. It's called "eye-tracking" and is done with a computer that sweeps back and forth on a screen to measure eye movement. Remember, the eyes are often referred to as "the windows of the mind."

One of the most astonishing research studies is going on at the University of Washington. They suspect that the nerves in your teeth—and there are thousands of sensory receptors in every tooth—may have a lot to do with the way you sense the world around you, same as do your eyes and ears and the taste buds in your tongue. The implication is that if you've lost your teeth, it could affect your perception of the world.

Dr. Lee R. Steiner, the New York psychologist mentioned in a previous chapter, has been doing extensive work with Kirlian Photography, a way of capturing luminous emanations from human fingertips directly on film. She has found these mysterious coronas correlate with brain function and is using them to treat brains overwhelmed by more stress than they can handle.

Dr. Dolores Krieger, a professor of nursing at New York University, has modified the mystical "laying on of hands" technique to heal and to reduce anxiety without any religious implications. She calls it the "Therapeutic Touch," practices it and teaches it.

She says that no special talent is required of the healer, only a deep desire to help the patient. When the hands are passed over the patient's body, from head to feet, almost but not quite touching the patient, the interaction reportedly boosts the patient's own recuperative powers to alleviate anxiety.

Probably the ultimate experience in mind control is a technique called "The Firewalk," which is based loosely on the theory that the brain undergoes a biochemical change that somehow influences the molecular arrangement of the soles of the feet.

You are asked to walk across 12 feet of hot coals in your bare feet without getting burned or blistered, and it is said that you can do so if your "mind-set" is correct. And if you can do so, you can turn "fear into power" and never fear anything again. When it was introduced recently in New York City, many who did "The Firewalk" said that it did indeed drive away their fear.

But it is not only new research and new techniques that give phobia sufferers an extra edge, there is also a very special group of people who are . . .

Phobic "Helpers"

Anyone who is phobic knows how important it is to have access to a support person with whom they can communicate and from whom they can get encouragement as they take steps to overcome their phobia.

So never be ashamed to ask for help from a spouse, lover, relative or friend. And if that someone has himself or herself recovered from a phobia, that would be the ideal person to seek support from.

You, and your helper, both gain from such an alliance.

You feel relief at being able to trust someone to whom you can surrender some control without feeling helpless, and your helper feels good about himself or herself for being given that trust.

A caring helper can let you out of the pressure cooker you might find yourself in if your fear level is high by giving you opportunities to let off steam without feeling embarrassed. If you find yourself getting panicky when you're half-way across a footbridge, tell your helper how you feel. This might cause you to retrace your steps and start all over again, or it might take the steam out of your panicky feelings and allow you to go across as you'd planned.

A good helper is someone who never pooh-poohs your fears, never tells you your complaints are "crazy," and never forces you to push yourself beyond your psychic ability.

A good helper's favorite words are: "I understand."

The helper's role is to nurture, not to nag, to give encouragement, not orders. And when the helper is a recovering phobic, lending support to another phobic can relieve his or her own apprehensiveness.

This kind of mutual support is especially helpful in dealing with agoraphobia.

"I couldn't walk out the door," says Pat. "I opened it for my husband when he left for work in the morning and when he came home at the end of the day. The door was as far as I could go until my husband began to help me."

What did he do?

"Not very much," he says matter-of-factly, "except maybe to show more interest in her, how she was doing, and compliment her for doing just a little bit more, even if that meant only crossing over the doorsill. When that happened, we both laughed, and that seemed to help, too."

A cooperative spouse can indeed be a good helper. Unfortunately, not all spouses are willing to be that cooperative. If the marriage is already a bit rocky, there is reason to suspect that one's spouse prefers to encourage the phobia rather than the cure.

Consider the case of Jim and Charlotte. She is absolutely terrified of flying. He, on the other hand, must fly because it's his job to pay regular visits to his company's branch offices around the country.

He never says so, but secretly he is delighted that his wife will not fly. His secretary is much better company and he always takes her along.

It keeps the marriage working, but it reinforces Charlotte's phobia every time Jim flies away, even though she doesn't know who's going along with him in her place!

When nothing is done to help overcome a phobia, it just keeps getting worse. Not only doesn't Jim help Charlotte, he has made her a victim of his philandering.

It works the other way around as well for some couples. Take the case of Ronnie and Marsha. He is terrified of thunder to the point of collapsing in shaky, sweaty, heart-pounding fear upon hearing a bolt of thunder even when he's safe at home and in bed.

She is terribly ashamed of his lack of "masculinity," because that is how she interprets his phobic symptoms. However, she is really pleased by what she considers a sign of weakness in him because this gives her a reason to show her contempt for him. She hasn't had any feeling for him for years and is staying married only because he is financially successful and so wrapped up in his work that he doesn't suspect her of having other lovers.

A cautionary note is advisable here. Rare as it may be, there are times when volunteering to be a phobic helper can backfire. It happened to Evelyn, who considered herself a good neighbor and acted on that assumption.

When her next door neighbor's home was robbed by an intruder who broke in one night and escaped with many valuables, but without being detected, the near-hysterical neighbor complained of her anxiety and fear to Evelyn who tried to placate her and help her overcome any further development of her fear.

Well, the neighbor told everybody, not just Evelyn, what had happened, and almost magically her fears disappeared. But Evelyn was not so fortunate.

"She got over it and I became phobic," said Evelyn. "Somehow, just listening to her tell me about the incident made me become fearful. I found myself afraid suddenly to do things that never frightened me before . . . taking an elevator alone, riding a subway, staying home alone at night.

"She was robbed and felt fine. I wasn't robbed, wasn't even threatened, and was phobic. If I'd stayed away from her and hadn't tried to help her, I'd never have caught her phobia!"

Caught her phobia?

Well, it could happen, but it's very unlikely. Phobias are not contagious. Some people, however, could be more susceptible than others.

For these, it may make good sense to seek out a professional helper. Many phobia clinics such as Phobia Associates in New York City have "outreach programs" for agoraphobic sufferers who need help desperately but cannot even leave their home to find such help. Like the doctors of yesteryear, they make "house calls" and send a professionally trained phobic helper to the client's home.

Available too are phobic helpers who make contact by telephone or letter. Members of the Phobia Society of America, TERRAP and other organizations can list their addresses and phone numbers in newsletters or reply to those already listed and thus make contact with a helping person.

You can avail yourself of Pen Pals, telephone Hot-Lines, or opt for group-counseling at a phobia clinic. All these ways lead to a sharing of phobic concerns and this alone can help to de-mystify their significance.

In group sessions, phobic parents often meet separately from their phobic youngsters, mostly teenagers, and spell out their feelings separately to the leader of the group. Often, this helps to bring about mutual understanding and the release of pent-up emotional feelings that contributed to the formation of the phobia in the first place.

"Just knowing that you are not the only person with this terrible affliction and that help is available is in itself tremendously therapeutic," says psychotherapist Jerilyn Ross, a recovered phobic herself.

True indeed. But there is something more to re-assure phobics that they are not alone. It's a very important something and not very much publicized, and is known by various names under the umbrella title of . . .

Mutual Self-Help Groups

Empathy, not sympathy, is the equalizer that links one phobia sufferer with another. As a special communications paper from the National Institute of Mental Health explains, "There is a special bond among people who share the same troubling experience; it begins when one person says to another, 'I know *just* how you feel.'

"Knowing that someone else truly understands one's feelings by virtue of having 'been there' brings a sense of relief."

The best known of such groups is probably Alcoholics Anonymous. Many men and women who try to drown their phobic fears in booze and beer attend A.A. meetings to cure their alcoholism.

However, that doesn't get to the heart of the real problem, which is phobia. They would do well to make use of the strategies and techniques described in this book and join a group of fellow phobics, if that is the reason for their drinking problem.

Phobias could also have a lot to do with anorexia nervosa, whose victims have an unrelenting, unrealistic fear of getting fat when in fact they continue to lose weight.

And people who can't seem to control urinating whenever they laugh, sneeze or cough may become anxious to a phobic degree that keeps them from going anywhere. But biofeedback, a technique known as Kegel exercises, and other methods might help them overcome the stress incontinence that caused them to become phobic.

The common denominator that ties all the above, as well as other afflictions, together is phobia, a rising tide of anxiety and a growing sense of panic. Luckily, there are numerous mutual self-help groups throughout the nation that deal with such afflictions and with specific phobic concerns.

In Part Three of this book, following this chapter, you will find a comprehensive *Phobia Resource Directory* that will list these groups and also Self-Help Clearinghouses nationwide that can provide you with further referrals, hotlines and other information.

The Clearinghouse is a major phenomenon in the grassroots growth of mutual self-help groups in America. In 1981, Edward

J. Madara, an idealistic sociologist, founded and assumed the directorship of the first computerized statewide self-help clearinghouse in the nation—New Jersey Self-Help Clearinghouse, St. Claire's Hospital Community Mental Health Center, Denville, New Jersey.

"Some self-help groups," he says, "are run for profit. They are effective but you have to sign up with a phobia clinic to participate.

"Our prime interest is in the self-help groups that are not commercial. They charge no fees, only minimal dues if any, and are run by the members of the group."

In a survey he conducted among the phobia groups in his bailiwick, he found that mutual support included group field trips, telephone support, a buddy system, an outreach program, an exposure/interaction program for new members and recovering agoraphobics, therapy recommendations and, above all, an agreed promise of confidentiality.

And he is excited about the possibility of extending mutual support via the computer that makes use of national computer networks like CompuServe. Meetings take place at the computer keyboard and screen. It's a high-tech extension of the mutual self-help concept.

Or, as computer expert Martin Lasden described it in *The New York Times,* "It's thought matched up against thought in what has been described as the closest thing to an incorporeal meeting of the minds."

But there are many who distrust the computer and who, some say, suffer from *techno-phobia.* Humorist Russell Baker, in a recent *New York Times* column, expressed great concern about his words disappearing from his computer screen because of a sudden, unexpected malfunction, and admitted, "I began to have the fear."

Well, he is not alone. A lot of people are beginning to have the fear, not of computers but of such highly publicized matters as Alzheimer's Disease, toxic waste build-up, contaminants in the food we eat, AIDS, and nuclear power, to name just a few contemporary scares.

If you take such matters personally and allow your imagination to play on the baleful effects of these perceived threats to your personal well-being, you are sure to magnify their potentially devastating effects. In short, instead of having a very low-level concern about these things, you will allow your mind to greatly exaggerate their possible threatening aspects.

Here is a *Worry Chart* based on a principle deduced by Natalie Schor, director of the Phobia & Anxiety Clinic at St. Luke's-Roosevelt Hospital Center in New York City, that can help you distinguish what is going on in your head from what is going on in the real world around you. And we're going to call it . . .

The Inside-Outside Self-Test

In phobia language, anxiety levels are measured from 1, the lowest, to 10, the highest. Using numbers instead of words takes some of the fearsome imagery out of what they signify.

Also, knowing that 10 is the highest you can go serves to reassure you that your phobic fear does indeed have its limits. (Review *Your Dread Degree* Self-Test in Chapter 4.)

All well and good. But the real problem, as Natalie Schor discovered, is resolved only when you become able to properly rate what's going on *inside* your head against what you see as going on *outside* your head.

How can you know?

On a 1-to-10 scale, measure the *percentage* of attention you're paying to *internal* events—everything from feeling dizzy, imagining disastrous happenings, and suffering from palpitations to feeling weak-kneed and on the verge of panic.

And on the same 1-to-10 scale, measure the *percentage* of attention you're giving to *external* events—what you actually see, hear, taste, whatever is actually going on outside of your mind.

In view of what you already know about levels of phobic anxiety, mark off on the chart that follows what percent of your attention is fixed on *internal* events and what percent of your attention is fixed on *external* events.

You will learn that if, for example, about 50 percent of your attention is fixed on internal events, as described above, and an equivalent 50 percent on external events, then you have reached an Anxiety Level of 5. That is halfway between the upper limit of Panic and the lower limit of Comfort.

But if you score yourself at, say, only 20 percent on internal events and score the rest of your attention, 80 percent, on external realities, your Anxiety Level is only 2, which should let you feel quite comfortable.

Now measure yourself against this *Worry Chart* . . .

Anxiety Level	=	*Internal Focus*	*vs.*	*External Focus*
10 (Panic Level)		100%		0%
9		90%		10%
8		80%		20%
7		70%		30%
6		60%		40%
5 (Even Up)		50%		50%
4		40%		60%
3		30%		70%
2		20%		80%
1 (Comfort Level)		0%		100%

You can see now that if you focus internally on your symptoms and scary thoughts, you are going to reach a higher level of anxiety. Perhaps this little self-test can help you make yourself more aware of external events—the reality around you, not the fantasy inside you—and help you bring down your phobic symptoms to easily manageable proportions.

Mutual self-help groups can make you mindful of the need to separate internal from external events. So, too, can a page-by-page referral to appropriate sections of this book, and the comprehensive Index will help you to pinpoint those pages that fit your particular needs.

While you are practicing the strategies and techniques described, try hard to remember to stay in the present, the here-

and-now. Keep to a single-minded purpose, and be content with taking small steps, one at a time, to overcome whatever fears might constitute your phobia.

Keep in mind the importance of saying what you mean. If you want something, for example, don't beat around the bush because you're afraid to express yourself and then get upset because no one understood clearly what you meant.

Phobias can be crippling, but they are beatable. You have learned of many ways to fight against fear, with strategies that work for the moment, and with powerful fear-fighting techniques that demolish phobic terrors permanently.

Do it yourself, or do it with help. But do it!

Now, not tomorrow—don't put it off—now is the right time to rid yourself of phobias, anxieties and panic attacks forever.

You know it can be done, in a multitude of ways. And remember, it is a fight that *you can win.*

You can take your finger off the panic button for good.

PART THREE

PHOBIA RESOURCE DIRECTORY (Nationwide)

Key Contacts in the Phobia Network

A VAST NETWORK of specialists in phobias, panic disorders and anxiety-related conditions is available to any reader who seeks further help. Here is a comprehensive listing of many kinds of professional resources, complete with addresses and telephone numbers (correct as of this writing), to which you can turn should you want . . .

To learn more about a particular technique or treatment.

To consult any of the experts mentioned in this book.

To join a self-help support group.

To find a phobia pen pal or dial-a-phobia hotline.

To visit a phobia clinic or join a research program.

Moreover, since this Resource Directory is intended to be as comprehensive as possible, some of the above entries will include cross-references to other entries that connect with the one that especially interests you. By this means, you are able to broaden your contacts or to learn more about them.

And don't forget to consult the Index at the back of this book if you want to refresh your memory about any subject. It will direct you to the precise page on which to find whatever information you're looking for.

Specialized Techniques and Treatment

ALEXANDER TECHNIQUE

Alexander Technique Affiliates
Linda Babits & Hillary Mayers
220 West 98th Street
New York, N.Y. 10025
Telephone: 212-866-8233 or 212-865-0556

Carnegie-Mellon University
Communications Specialist Pamela Lewis
5017 Forbes Avenue
Pittsburgh, Penna. 15213
Telephone: 412-578-2900

ANTI-PANIC PHARMACOLOGY

New York State Psychiatric Institute
Columbia-Presbyterian Medical Center
722 West 168th Street
New York, N.Y. 10032
Telephone: 212-960-2367 or 2368

BIOFEEDBACK

Associated Biofeedback Medical Group (Also HYPNOSIS)
Elliot Wineburg, M.D.
30 Central Park South
New York, N.Y. 10019
Telephone: 212-308-1368

Biofeedback Developmental Center
Howard E. Kay, B.C.I.A.
One Station Square
Forest Hills, N.Y. 11375
Telephone: 718-263-9388

FEARFUL FLYER TAPES AND GROUPS

Soar (HOME-STUDY CASSETTES and GROUP SEMINARS)

Capt. Tom Bunn
P.O. Box 747
Westport, Conn. 06881
Telephone: 800-332-7359 (800-FEARFLY) or 203-259-9987

Freedom From Fear of Flying (GROUPS ONLY)
2021 Country Club Prado
Coral Gables, Fla. 33134
Telephone: 305-261-7042

Many airlines offer course. Check for yourself.

Experts and Specialists

DENNIS BAREK, M.D. (Esthetic Cosmetic Surgery)
10 East 88th Street
New York, N.Y. 10028
Telephone: 212-289-5281

JULIAN M. HERSKOWITZ, Ph.D. (Director of TERRAP, N.Y.)
356 New York Avenue
Huntington, Long Island, N.Y. 11743
Telephone: 516-549-8867

On the West Coast, your contact would be:
Arthur B. Hardy, M.D.
TERRAP
1010 Doyle Drive
Menlo Park, Calif. 94025
Telephone 415-329-1233 or 800-2-PHOBIA

EDWIN D. JOY, D.D.S. (Dental Phobia)
Medical College of Georgia
Augusta, Ga. 30902
Telephone: 404-828-2411

MARSHALL P. PRIMACK, M.D. (Diagnostic Medicine)
842 Park Avenue
New York, N.Y. 10021
Telephone: 212-879-1666

JERILYN ROSS, M.A. (Clinician and Educator)
Roundhouse Square Psychiatric Center
Associate Director
Alexandria, Va. 22313
Telephone: 703-836-7130

DAVID SHEEHAN, M.D. (Anxiety Disease)
Panic and Phobia Disorders Clinic
University of South Florida Medical Center
Dept. of Psychiatry and Behavioral Medicine
12901 North 30th Street
Box 33
Tampa, Fla. 33612
Telephone: 813-974-3374

Self-Help Support Groups

As described in Chapter 8, self-help groups are composed of people who share a common fear and join together for mutual support. The members themselves run the group. Most solicit only contributions in the form of minimal dues. Some publish their own newsletters; some maintain a hotline service.

While most deal with phobias of all kinds, there are those that restrict themselves to one kind of phobia in particular, such as . . .

AGORAPHOBIA
Agoraphobia Support/Travel Group
CUNY Graduate Center
33 West 42nd Street (Room 1222)
New York, N.Y. 10036
Telephone: 212-556-1371

Agoraphobic Action Phone Line
Telephone: 212-231-3056

Agoraphobia Group
St. Clare's Hospital
Pocono Road
Denville, N.J. 07834
Telephone: 201-625-9565

Agoraphobics In Motion
605 W. 11 Mile Rd.
Royal Oak, Mich. 48067
Telephone: 313-547-0400
(Groups also meet elsewhere in Michigan and Glens Falls, N.Y.)

Of course many of the clinics and treatment centers listed in this directory offer Agoraphobia groups that meet under *professional* auspices. But those listed above are run by the phobics themselves as explained in the previous chapter.

Now here are some self-help support groups that deal with . . .

PHOBIC FEAR AND ANXIETY

Emotions Anonymous International
P.O. Box 4245
St. Paul, Minn. 55104
Telephone: 612-647-9712

Neurotics Anonymous
P.O. Box 4866
Cleveland Park Station
Washington, D.C. 20008
Telephone: 202-232-0414

Recovery Inc.
802 North Dearborn Street
Chicago, Illinois 60610
Telephone: 312-337-5661

The above-mentioned contacts are national headquarters. They can put you in touch with groups in your area, or you can check your local phone directory first.

The role played by the *Self-Help Clearinghouse* was described in Chapter 8. Most, but not all, states have such Clearinghouses that dispense information about self-help support groups. If there is none where you live, you can contact the national center for everything about where to find a support group to how to organize one . . .

The National Self-Help Clearinghouse
33 West 42nd Street (Room 1227)
New York, N.Y. 10036
Attention: Frank Riessman, Director
Telephone: 212-840-1259

You may find this step unnecessary, however, if your state appears in the following list of Self-Help Clearinghouses and Associations. All addresses and phone numbers are accurate as of this writing. If you can't find what you want here, check your local telephone directory or the national office. Here is a state-by-state breakdown:

CALIFORNIA

California Self-Help Center
U.C.L.A. Psychology Department
405 Hilgard Avenue
Los Angeles, Calif. 90024
Telephone: 213-825-1799, or 1-800-222-LINK

Merced County Self-Help Clearinghouse
Mental Health Association
P.O. Box 343
Merced, Calif. 95341
Telephone: 209-723-8861

Sacramento Self-Help Clearinghouse
Mental Health Association

5370 Elvas Avenue (Suite B)
Sacramento, Calif. 95819
Telephone: 916-456-2070

San Diego Self-Help Clearinghouse
P.O. Box 86246
San Diego, Calif. 92138-6246
Telephone: 619-275-2344

San Francisco Self-Help Clearinghouse
Mental Health Association
2398 Pine Street
San Francisco, Calif. 94115
Telephone: 415-921-4401

CONNECTICUT

Connecticut Self-Help Mutual Support Network
Consultation Center
19 Howe Street
New Haven, Conn. 06511
Telephone: 203-789-7645

ILLINOIS

Self-Help Center
1600 Dodge Avenue (Suite S-122)
Evanston, Illinois 60201
Telephone: 312-328-0470

KANSAS

Self-Help Center of Kansas
P.O. Box 8511
Wichita, Kansas 67208
Telephone: 316-686-1205

MASSACHUSETTS

Cooperative Extension Service
Division of Home Economics
University of Massachusetts
113 Skinner Hall
Amherst, Mass. 01003
Telephone: 413-545-2715

MICHIGAN

Michigan Self-Help Clearinghouse
Riverwood Community Mental Health Center
512 Ship Street
St. Joseph, Michigan 49085
Telephone: 616-983-0343

MINNESOTA

Community Care Unit
Minnesota Mutual Help Resource Center
Wilder Foundation
919 Lafond Avenue
St. Paul, Minn. 55104
Telephone: 612-642-4060

MISSOURI

Support Group Clearinghouse
Kansas City Assn. for Mental Health
Kansas City, MO. 64110
Telephone: 816-361-5007

NEBRASKA

Self-Help Information Services
1601 Euclid Avenue
Lincoln, Nebraska 68502
Telephone: 402-476-9668

NEW JERSEY

New Jersey Self-Help Clearinghouse
St. Clare's-Riverside Medical Center
Denville, N.J. 07834
Telephone: 201-625-9565 (In N.J.: 1-800-FOR-MASH)
(The director, Edward J. Madara, is a trailblazer in mutual self-help groups and maintains a comprehensive computerized listing of hundreds of groups and information on how to set up a group)

NEW YORK

New York State Self-Help Clearinghouse
N.Y. Council on Children & Families
Empire State Plaza, Tower 2
Albany, N.Y. 12224

Telephone: 518-474-6293
(Maintains list of self-help groups in upstate New York)

Brooklyn Self-Help Clearinghouse
Heights Hills Mental Health Service
30 3rd Avenue
Brooklyn, N.Y. 11217
Telephone: 718-834-7341 or 7332

New York City Self-Help Clearinghouse, Inc.
1012 Eighth Avenue
Brooklyn, N.Y. 11215
Telephone: 718-788-8787

Long Island Self-Help Clearinghouse
New York Institute of Technology
Central Islip Campus
Central Islip, N.Y. 11722
Telephone: 516-348-3030

Orange County Dept. of Mental Health
Consultation and Education Dept.
Harriman Drive, Drawer 471
Goshen, N.Y. 10925
Telephone: 914-294-6185

Niagara Self-Help Clearinghouse
151 East Avenue
Lockport, N.Y. 14094
Telephone: 716-433-3780

Rockland County CMHC
Sanitorium Road
Pomona, N.Y. 10970
Telephone: 914-354-0200

Westchester Community College

Academic Arts Building
75 Grasslands Avenue
Valhalla, N.Y. 10595
Telephone: 914-347-3620

OREGON

N.W. Regional Self-Help Clearinghouse
718 West Burnside Street
Portland, Oregon 97209
Telephone: 503-222-5555 or 226-9360

PENNSYLVANIA

JFK Community Mental Health Center
112 N. Broad Street
Philadelphia, Penna. 19102
Telephone: 215-568-0860

Self-Help Group Network
2839 Beechwood Boulevard
Pittsburgh, Penna. 15217
Telephone: 412-521-9822

Self-Help Information & Networking Exchange (SHINE)
Voluntary Action Center of N.E. Pennsylvania
200 Adams Avenue
Scranton, Penna. 18503
Telephone: 717-961-1234

TENNESSEE

Overlook Mental Health Center
6906 Kingston Pike
Knoxville, Tenn. 36919
Telephone: 615-588-9747

TEXAS

Dallas Self-Help Clearinghouse
Mental Health Association of Dallas County
2500 Maple Avenue
Dallas, Texas 75201-1998
Telephone: 214-871-2420

Tarrant County Self-Help Clearinghouse
Mental Health Association of Tarrant County
3136 West 4th Street
Fort Worth, Texas 76107-2113
Telephone: 817-335-5405

VERMONT

Vermont Self-Help Clearinghouse
c/o Parents Anonymous
P.O. Box 829
Montpelier, Vt. 05602
Telephone: 802-229-5724 (In Vermont: 1-800-544-5030)

WASHINGTON, D.C.

Greater Washington Self-Help Coalition
Mental Health Association of Northern Virginia
100 N. Washington Street, Suite 232
Falls Church, Virginia 22046
Telephone: 703-536-4100
(Includes Washington, D.C., northern Virginia and southern Maryland)

WASHINGTON STATE

Crisis Clinic of Thurston and Mason Counties
P.O. Box 2463
Olympia, Washington 98507
Telephone: 206-352-2211 or 426-3311

WISCONSIN

Continuing Education in Mental Health
University of Wisconsin Extension
414 Lowell Hall
610 Langden Street
Madison, Wisc. 53706
Telephone: 608-263-4432

Mutual Aid Self-Help Association (MASHA)
P.O. Box 09304
Milwaukee, Wisc. 53211
Telephone: 414-461-1466

CANADA

Self-Help Clearinghouse
CAMAC, Inc.
3737 Vanhorne
Montreal, Quebec, Canada
H3S 1R9
Telephone: 514-341-1440

Quite apart from the above support groups is a very special group that deals with . . .

SEX PHOBIAS

A unique support group, led by professionals, has been started at the Michael Reese Medical Center in Chicago. It is composed of sexually impotent men of all ages and is led by urologist Leon Lome, M.D., and psychologist Jonathan Scott, Ph.D., in a group program called SIR (Sexual Impotency Resolved), and sexual fears are explored in a support group setting. Other medical institutions may have similar support groups. Inquire locally, or contact . . .

Michael Reese Hospital & Medical Center
SIR (Dept. of Urology)
Lake Shore Drive at 31st Street
Chicago, Illinois 60616
Telephone: 312-791-2297

Pen Pals and Hotlines

PHOBIA SOCIETY OF AMERICA (Also has Newsletter and Local Chapters Nationwide)

133 Rollins Avenue, Suite 4B
Rockville, Md. 20852-4004

Send a self-addressed, stamped, legal-sized envelope for information on how to join and how to find a Pen Pal. You can ask for a phobic person, a recovered phobic, or a family member of a phobic person.

TERRAP (TERRitorial APprehensiveness)
National Headquarters (Also offers Correspondence Course)
1010 Dyle Street
Menlo Park, Calif. 94025
Telephone 415-329-1233 or 800-2-PHOBIA

Ask about access to a Pen Pal network or a telephone Hotline network. On the East coast, the Long Island TERRAP center maintains such services. You can contact the director, Dr. Julian M. Herskowitz, at the address listed previously under Experts and Specialists.

PHOBIC HOTLINE
215-47 47th Avenue
Bayside, N.Y. 11361
Telephone: 718-224-3345

While this Hotline is most practical for readers who reside within or near its geographical area, similar Hotlines exist in all sections of the United States and Canada. To locate one, first check your local telephone directory, then the directory of the city nearest you. Look under these headings: Phobia Hotline, Phobic Hotline, Phobia Lifeline and Phobic Lifeline.

SEX PHOBIA HOTLINES
If you are fearful about AIDS, Herpes or other V.D. conditions, here are National Toll-free numbers to call . . .

V.D. National Hotline
American Social Health Association
National: 1-800-227-8922
In California: 1-800-982-5883

AIDS Hotline
National Public Health Service
National: 1-800-342-AIDS or 1-800-443-0366
In Atlanta: 404-329-1296

800 AIDS Information
National Gay/Lesbian Task Force Crisisline
National: 1-800-221-7044
In New York: 212-529-1604

Clinics, Medical Centers and Treatment Programs

Some in the following list sponsor professionally led support groups; some publish newsletters; and some conduct research on panic disorder and various phobic conditions for which volunteers are invited to participate for innovative experimental treatment without fee. Ask about such matters if they interest you. And if you reside in a large city, check the Public Notices column of your Sunday newspaper for announcements of special research programs being offered at nearby medical facilities.

Please bear in mind that telephone numbers, addresses and even programs are subject to change, but at this writing the list that follows is accurate. And where there is something special about this or that listing, a note to that effect has been appended.

ARIZONA

Behavioral Health Center
St. Luke's Medical Center
Pain and Stress Clinic
1800 E. Van Buren Street
Phoenix, Arizona 85006
Telephone: 602-251-8790

CALIFORNIA

USC-Los Angeles County Medical Center
Anxiety Disorders Clinic
1937 Hospital Place

Los Angeles, Calif. 90033
Telephone: 213-226-5329

New Beginning Foundation (Audio Cassettes for Agoraphobia)
P.O. Box 15519
North Hollywood, CA 91615
Telephone: 818-780-3110

CONNECTICUT

Yale Psychiatric Institute
Huntington and Prospect Streets
P.O. Box 12A—Yale Station
New Haven, Conn. 06520
Telephone: 203-436-1519

FLORIDA

Agoraphobia Resource Center
2699 S. Bayshore Dr.—Suite 800E
Coconut Grove, Fla. 33313
Telephone: 305-854-0652

University of Miami School of Medicine
Dept. of Psychiatry
Box 016960
Miami, Fla. 33101
Telephone: 305-549-6335

Panic and Phobia Disorders Clinic (Tampa)
(See David Sheehan, M.D./Anxiety Disease listing under Experts and Specialists)

ILLINOIS

Rush-Presbyterian-St. Luke's Medical Center
1725 West Harrison Street—Suite 1074
Chicago, Illinois 60612
Telephone: 312-942-0118

Phobia Clinic
Dept. of Psychiatry
University of Chicago

5841 S. Maryland Avenue
Chicago, Illinois 60637
Telephone: 312-962-9726

IOWA

Department of Psychiatry
University of Iowa
500 Newton Road
Iowa City, Iowa 52242
Telephone: 319-353-5422

LOUISIANA

Tulane University Medical School
Dept. of Psychiatry and Neurology
1430 Tulane Avenue
New Orleans, La. 70112
Telephone: 504-588-5246

MARYLAND

Thomas W. Uhde, M.D.
Unit on Anxiety and Affective Disorders
National Institute of Mental Health
9000 Rockville Pike
Building 10—Room 3S-239
Bethesda, Md. 20205
Telephone: 301-496-6825

MASSACHUSETTS

Agoraphobia Treatment Center of New England
264 Beacon Street
Boston, Mass. 02116
Telephone: 617-262-5223

Anxiety Research Clinic
Massachusetts General Hospital
15 Parkman Street
ACC-717
Boston, Mass. 02114
Telephone: 617-726-3488

MICHIGAN

Anxiety Disorders Program

Dept. of Psychiatry
University of Michigan Hospitals
Ann Arbor, Mich. 48109
Telephone: 313-764-5348

NEW JERSEY

Agoraphobia Clinic of N.J., P.A.
1388 Palisade Avenue
Fort Lee, N.J. 07024
Telephone: 201-944-8956 or 444-2878

NEW YORK

Phobia and Anxiety Disorders Clinic
State University of New York
1535 Western Avenue
Albany, N.Y. 12203
Telephone: 518-456-4127

Phobia Clinic
Hillside Hospital, Long Island Jewish Medical Center
75-59 263rd Street
Glen Oaks, N.Y. 11004
Telephone: 718-470-8120

Phobia Associates, Inc. (Offers Outreach program)
81 Grand Street
New York, N.Y. 10013
Telephone: 212-226-6804
(Therapists make house calls to agoraphobes who cannot leave their homes, everywhere in the five boroughs of New York City and in areas of Long Island, Westchester and Long Island)

Michael R. Liebowitz, M.D.
Anxiety Disorders Clinic
New York State Psychiatric Institute
722 West 168th Street
New York, N.Y. 10032
Telephone: 212-960-2367 or 2368
(Often offers free treatment to those between ages 18–55, in

good medical health, no alcoholism or drug abuse, and suffering from general anxiety, phobias, or panic attacks, and willing to participate in research)

Affective Disorders Clinic
Department of Psychiatry
University of Rochester
300 Crittenden Boulevard
Rochester, N.Y. 14642
Telephone: 716-275-7818

Anxiety Disorders Unit
Payne Whitney Clinic
New York Hospital-Cornell Medical Center
525 East 68th Street
New York, N.Y. 10021
Telephone: 212-472-4862

Phobia Clinic
White Plains Hospital Medical Center
Davis Avenue at East Post Road
White Plains, N.Y. 10601
Telephone: 914-681-1078

Phobia and Anxiety Disorders Program
St. Luke's-Roosevelt Hospital Center
36 West 60th Street
New York, N.Y. 10023
Telephone: 212-554-7172

NORTH CAROLINA

Anxiety, Panic and Phobia Disorders Program
Highland Hospital
49 Zillicoa Street
Asheville, N.C. 28802
Telephone: 704-254-3201

PENNSYLVANIA

Agoraphobia and Anxiety Program

Temple University Medical School
112 Bala Avenue
Bala Cynwyd, Penna. 19004
Telephone: 215-667-6490

Friends Hospital
Department of Psychology
Ronald Coleman, Ph.D.
Roosevelt Boulevard and Adams Avenue
Philadelphia, Penna. 19124
Telephone: 215-831-4600

SOUTH CAROLINA

Anxiety Disorders Clinic
Dept. of Psychiatry
Medical University of South Carolina
171 Ashley Avenue
Charleston, S.C. 29425
Telephone: 803-792-2010

TEXAS

Anxiety Disorder Research Group (Prominent in Research)
Barry Fenton, M.D.
University of Texas Health Science Center
5323 Harry Hines Boulevard
Dallas, Texas 75235
Telephone: 214-688-3240
(People in the North Texas area who suffer from panic attacks may be eligible for free treatment in on-going research studies on this disorder)

UTAH

University of Utah Medical Center
Dept. of Psychiatry
50 North Medical Drive
Salt Lake City, Utah 84132
Telephone: 801-581-8075

WISCONSIN

Center for Health Sciences
Dept. of Psychiatry

University of Wisconsin
600 Highland Avenue
Madison, Wisc. 53792
Telephone: 608-263-6075

For Additional Information or Professional Referrals

To find a local practitioner in the field of psychiatry or psychology, you might first try telephoning your local Mental Health Association and request a referral to a phobia specialist. Or you can contact one of their professional associations directly:

American Psychiatric Association
1400 K. Street, N.W.
Washington, D.C. 20005
Telephone: 202-797-4900

American Psychological Association
1200 Seventeenth Street, N.W.
Washington, D.C. 20036
Telephone: 202-833-7600

You can also consult the Yellow Pages of your telephone directory under such headings as "Phobias," "Psychotherapy" and "Counseling Services." But before undergoing treatment, be sure to double-check the legitimacy and expertise of the individual or group that interests you. The local Mental Health Association should be able to help you.

By and large, however, you should be able to find an appropriate person to consult within this Resource Directory. All mentioned herein are top-drawer experts in their field.

If you don't have a personal physician, ask the nearest hospital to recommend one. To locate the nearest specialist in family medicine, contact:

The American Academy of Family Physicians
1740 West 92nd Street

Kansas City, MO 64114
Telephone: 800-821-2512, or 816-333-9700

Finally, if you are phobic about the environment, the food you eat or health matters in general, you might want to seek information from these consumer education groups . . .

American Council on Science and Health
1995 Broadway
New York, N.Y. 10023
Telephone: 212-362-7044

Center for Science in the Public Interest
1755 S Street, N.W.
Washington, D.C. 20004
Telephone: 202-332-9110

Index